SIMPLY STYLISH
DRESSING UP
PACKETS & CANS

CAROLYN HUMPHRIES

foulsham
LONDON • NEW YORK • TORONTO • SYDNEY

foulsham

The Publishing House, Bennetts Close,
Cippenham, Slough, Berkshire, SL1 5AP, England

ISBN 0-572-02467-3

Copyright © 1999 W. Foulsham & Co. Ltd

Printed in Great Britain by Cox & Wyman Ltd, Reading

CONTENTS

INTRODUCTION

How many times have you been to a dinner party and known that everything you had came from M&S or Sainsbury's? It's not the same as having something made especially for you, is it? But if you're up to your neck in work or running a home and family, or don't feel your culinary skills are up to much, there's no time or inclination to shop and cook for elaborate meals. And for every day, more and more of us are having to turn to convenience foods to save time. But they can be pretty boring.

Not any more! My plan was to create a range of delectable dishes for every occasion which could all be prepared in next to no time, with the minimum of effort, from ingredients that are always to hand – if you keep a well-stocked pantry (see page 5). The result is a book absolutely brimming with exciting ideas from light-as-air soufflés to sumptuous, sinful desserts. They're all made from cans, packets and some basic frozen foods, so you will always be able to make mouthwatering meals just like that. And no one will know you haven't spent hours slaving over a hot stove and gone to enormous expense ... unless you tell them.

THE WELL-STOCKED PANTRY

If you keep the following in your kitchen, you'll always be able to create a meal in a moment. These are not the only ingredients used in the book, but they form the basis of many delicious dishes. And as you discover new recipes you like, add their ingredients to your store.

Taste ticklers
- Tube of tomato purée (paste)
- Jar of passata (sieved tomatoes)
- Dried herbs: mixed are essential, plus mint, oregano, rosemary, basil, thyme, bay leaves and dill (dill weed), preferably
- Garlic powder, granules or purée
- Coarse ground black pepper
- Salt
- Mustard – Dijon, if only keeping one
- Vinegar – red wine, white wine or cider (no need for malt as well unless you prefer it)
- Stock cubes – vegetable essential, plus chicken and beef, preferably
- Spices – nutmeg, cinnamon, paprika, chilli or cayenne
- Curry paste or powder
- Redcurrant jelly (clear conserve)
- Sunflower oil – essential, plus olive oil preferably
- Sugar – caster (superfine) essential, plus light brown
- Dried milk (non-fat dry milk) and/or evaporated milk

- Carton UHT whipping cream and/or canned or frozen cream
- Lemon juice

Clever cans
- Tomatoes
- Tuna
- Sweetcorn (corn)
- Red kidney beans
- Minced (ground) or stewed steak
- Ham
- Condensed soups
- Fruit in natural juice
- Custard

Magic mixes
- White/cheese sauce
- Batter
- Bread sauce
- Lemon meringue pie
- Crème caramel
- Sponge cake

Fridge and freezer friends
- Medium eggs
- Cheddar cheese
- Grated Parmesan cheese
- Sunflower or olive oil spread (suitable for baking and spreading)
- Mayonnaise (I use a 'light' variety)
- Frozen pastry (paste): puff, filo and shortcrust (basic pie crust)
- Frozen peas
- Frozen prawns (shrimp)
- Fresh parsley (freeze in plastic bag, use from frozen)

Exceptional extras
- Pasta – any shape
- Long-grain rice
- Plain (all-purpose) flour
- Baking powder
- Cornflour (cornstarch)
- Part-baked French sticks or ciabatta bread

Vital veggies
- Potatoes
- Onions
- Carrots
- White cabbage (to cook or shred for salad)

HELP — I'VE RUN OUT OF ...

With even the best-laid plans, it's easy to run out of that vital little ingredient. Here are a few tips for alternatives you can use:

- Tomato purée (paste): use ketchup (catsup), passata (sieved tomatoes), canned or packet tomato soup – you'll be amazed what a cup-a-soup sprinkled into a casserole can do!

- Wine: use 1 part wine vinegar to 2 parts water. If the result is a little sharp, add a little sugar (2.5–5 ml/ ½–1 tsp should be sufficient). If you have a drop of sherry, vermouth or cider, these make good substitutes for wine in recipes.

- Stock cubes – chicken: 1 chicken cup-a-soup for up to 300 ml/½ pt/1¼ cups stock (chicken noodle is ideal and the noodles will cook out in the casserole) or Chicken Bovril (use sparingly). Beef: canned consommé is ideal, or Bovril (use sparingly), or oxtail cup-a-soup (see chicken). Vegetable: try Marmite or Vegemite (use sparingly), or vegetable cup-a-soup (see chicken). All: Brown table sauce/Worcestershire sauce/soy sauce can add flavour and colour too.

- Flour (for thickening soups, sauces and casseroles): crumble in a Weetabix, or add a little instant oat cereal or mashed potato powder a spoonful at a time, whisking in well.

- Sugar: if your recipe calls for caster (superfine) or icing (confectioners') sugar and all you have is granulated, tip it into the food processor and grind it down. If you have white sugar and your recipe calls for brown, add 5 ml/1 tsp or so of gravy browning to the mixture (you won't get quite the same flavour, but the colour will be right!)

- Chocolate: if you need plain (semi-sweet) chocolate or cocoa (unsweetened chocolate) powder and all you have is milk chocolate or drinking (sweetened) chocolate powder, add 2.5–5 ml/½–1 tsp instant coffee dissolved in the smallest amount of water to it. If the recipe calls for milk chocolate and you have plain (semi-sweet) only, add 15–30 ml/1–2 tbsp dried milk (non-fat dry milk) powder to any dry ingredients, or blend it with the smallest amount of warm water until smooth to add to 'wet' ingredients.

- Golden (light corn) syrup: clear honey can be substituted.

- Breadcrumbs as a topping or coating: crushed cornflakes/branflakes, porridge oats or, for a savoury coating, stuffing mix can be used instead.

NOTES ON THE RECIPES

- Use either metric, imperial or American measures for a recipe, not a combination.

- All spoon measures are level: 1 tsp = 5 ml
  1 tbsp = 15 ml

- Eggs are medium unless otherwise stated.

- Wash, dry, core, peel and seed, where necessary, all fresh produce before preparation unless otherwise stated.

- Preheat the oven and cook on the centre shelf unless otherwise stated.

- Most of the herbs used in this book are dried, for speed. The exception is parsley. Do not substitute dried parsley for fresh, it just won't taste right. Instead, keep a bag of fresh parsley in the freezer, then use from frozen as required.

- All preparation and cooking times at the end of recipes are approximate and cooking time refers to conventional cooking. If a microwave or pressure cooker is used instead (as sometimes suggested), then the times will be reduced considerably.

- All can sizes are approximate, as they vary slightly from brand to brand.

SOUPS

Hot or cold, thick or thin, a bowl of soup makes a delicious light meal or starter for a dinner party. Of course, you could just open a can – but the taste is rarely exciting. Don't settle for second-best. If you are really pushed for time, try mixing a can of cream of tomato soup with a can of chopped tomatoes. Spice it up with a spoonful of Worcestershire sauce, sprinkle with crisply fried (sautéed) croûtons and you have a Tomato Special. This just shows you that with a little inspiration you can create masterpieces!

Minted Pea Soup

SERVES 4	METRIC	IMPERIAL	AMERICAN
Frozen peas	225g	8 oz	8 oz
Vegetable or chicken stock	600 ml	1 pt	2½ cups
Dried mint	5 ml	1 tsp	1 tsp
Pinch of pepper			
Instant mashed potato (optional), to thicken	30 ml	2 tbsp	2 tbsp
Single (light) cream	150 ml	¼ pt	⅔ cup
Dried chives or dried mint, to garnish			

1 Cook the peas in the stock with the mint for 5 minutes.

2 Liquidise or sieve and return to the saucepan.

3 Season with a little pepper and whisk in the potato, if using.

4 Stir in all but 30 ml/2 tbsp of the cream.

5 Reheat but do not boil. Alternatively, chill, if preferred. Serve in soup bowls, garnished with a swirl of the reserved cream and a sprinkling of herbs.

PREPARATION TIME: 2 MINUTES

COOKING TIME: 5 MINUTES PLUS REHEATING OR CHILLING TIME

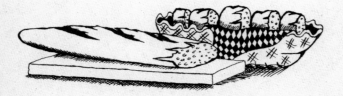

Tangy Carrot and Tomato Soup

SERVES 4	METRIC	IMPERIAL	AMERICAN
Can of carrots	275g	10 oz	1 small
Can of tomatoes	400 g	14 oz	1 large
Pure orange juice	150 ml	¼ pt	⅔ cup
Dried basil or mixed herbs	5 ml	1 tsp	1 tsp
Salt and pepper			
Plain yoghurt or a little cream (any will do), to serve	20 ml	4 tsp	4 tsp

1 Drain the carrots and place in a food processor or blender.

2 Add the contents of the can of tomatoes and blend until smooth. Alternatively, pass both through a sieve (strainer).

3 Add the orange juice, herbs and seasoning to taste.

4 Heat through or chill, and serve in bowls with 5 ml/1 tsp of yoghurt or cream spooned over each portion.

PREPARATION TIME:
2 MINUTES

COOKING TIME:
2 MINUTES OR
CHILLING TIME

Crab Bisque

SERVES 6	METRIC	IMPERIAL	AMERICAN
Onion, very finely chopped	1	1	1
Butter or margarine	25 g	1 oz	2 tbsp
Can of dressed crab	43 g	1¾ oz	1 small
Plain (all-purpose) flour	45 ml	3 tbsp	3 tbsp
Fish, chicken or vegetable stock	900 ml	1½ pts	3¾ cups
Celery salt	5 ml	1 tsp	1 tsp
Dry sherry	30 ml	2 tbsp	2 tbsp
Milk	150 ml	¼ pt	⅔ cup
Single (light) cream	150 ml	¼ pt	⅔ cup
Can of white crabmeat	170 g	6 oz	1 small
Croûtons (cubes of bread sautéed in oil), to garnish			

❁

1 Fry (sauté) the onion gently in the butter in a saucepan for 3 minutes until softened but not browned.

2 Stir in the dressed crab and the flour and cook for 1 minute.

3 Remove from the heat and gradually blend in the stock. Bring to the boil, stirring until thickened. Simmer for 15 minutes.

4 Stir in the remaining ingredients. Reheat but do not boil. Serve in soup bowls garnished with croûtons.

PREPARATION TIME:
2 MINUTES

COOKING TIME:
20 MINUTES

Rich Green Soup

Instead of frozen spinach and beans, you could use drained cans of beans and spinach and simmer for 5 minutes only. However, frozen gives better colour and flavour.

SERVES 6	METRIC	IMPERIAL	AMERICAN
Onion, chopped	1	1	1
Butter or margarine	15 g	½ oz	1 tbsp
Frozen broad (lima) beans	225 g	8 oz	8 oz
Frozen chopped spinach	225 g	8 oz	8 oz
Vegetable or chicken stock	900 ml	1½ pts	3¾ cups
Grated nutmeg	1.5 ml	¼ tsp	¼ tsp
Salt and pepper			
Crisp-cooked crumbled bacon (optional), to garnish			

1 Fry (sauté) the onion in the butter in a large saucepan for 3 minutes until softened but not browned.

2 Add the beans, spinach and stock.

3 Bring to the boil, reduce the heat, cover and simmer for 10 minutes or until the beans and onion are soft.

4 Pour into a food processor or blender and process until smooth, or pass through a sieve (strainer).

5 Season to taste with nutmeg, salt and pepper. Reheat and serve with the bacon sprinkled over, if liked.

PREPARATION TIME:
2 MINUTES

COOKING TIME:
10 MINUTES

Italian-style Consommé

SERVES 4	METRIC	IMPERIAL	AMERICAN
Elbow macaroni or other small soup pasta	40 g	1½ oz	1½ oz
Salt			
Can of condensed consommé	295 g	10½ oz	1 small
Red wine or port	30 ml	2 tbsp	2 tbsp
Grated Parmesan cheese, to serve			

1 Cook the pasta in plenty of boiling, salted water until tender. Drain and rinse with hot water.

2 Empty the consommé into a saucepan. Add water as directed and heat through. Stir in the wine or port and the pasta. Reheat.

3 Ladle into soup bowls and serve with grated Parmesan cheese.

PREPARATION TIME: 2 MINUTES COOKING TIME: 10 MINUTES

Chinese Egg Flower Soup

SERVES 4	METRIC	IMPERIAL	AMERICAN
Chicken stock	900 ml	1½ pts	3¾ cups
Soy sauce	15 ml	1 tbsp	1 tbsp
Dry sherry	30 ml	2 tbsp	2 tbsp
Pinch of ground ginger			
Frozen peas	25 g	1 oz	1 oz
Egg, beaten	1	1	1
Prawn crackers (optional), to serve			

1 Put all the ingredients except the egg in a saucepan and heat to boiling point.

2 Remove from the heat and pour the egg in a thin stream through the prongs of a fork, so it solidifies in 'flowers'.

3 Let the soup stand for 10 seconds for the egg to set, then ladle into soup bowls. Serve with prawn crackers, if liked.

PREPARATION TIME:
2 MINUTES

COOKING TIME:
3 MINUTES

Spanish Summer Soup

For convenience, red and green (bell) peppers can be frozen whole, then chopped for use as required.

SERVES 4	METRIC	IMPERIAL	AMERICAN
Slice of white bread	1	1	1
Lemon juice	15 ml	1 tbsp	1 tbsp
Small onion, roughly chopped	½	½	½
Small garlic clove, crushed (optional)	1	1	1
Lettuce leaves (use the outside ones you usually discard)	4	4	4
Piece of cucumber (the end will do)	5 cm	2 in	2 in
Red (bell) pepper (optional)	½	½	½
Olive oil	30 ml	2 tbsp	2 tbsp
Can of tomatoes	400 g	14 oz	1 large
Tomato purée (paste)	15 ml	1 tbsp	1 tbsp
Salt and pepper			
Pinch of caster (superfine) sugar			
Iced water	150 ml	¼ pt	⅔ cup
Cucumber slices (optional), to garnish			

1 Soak the bread in a little water for 1 minute. Squeeze out and place in a blender or food processor with all the other ingredients, except the iced water.

2 Run the machine until the mixture is blended. Stir in the iced water and serve in soup bowls. Float a slice of cucumber on each bowl, if liked.

PREPARATION TIME:
5 MINUTES

Monday Mulligatawny

This recipe is so-called because it utilises the vegetables left over from the Sunday roast.

SERVES 4	METRIC	IMPERIAL	AMERICAN
Cooked leftover (or frozen) mixed vegetables	225 g	8 oz	8 oz
Garlic clove, crushed	1	1	1
Curry paste	5–10 ml	1–2 tsp	1–2 tsp
Oil	15 ml	1 tbsp	1 tbsp
Vegetable stock	600 ml	1 pt	2½ cups
Tomato purée (paste)	15 ml	1 tbsp	1 tbsp
Instant mashed potato (optional), to thicken	15 ml	1 tbsp	1 tbsp
Salt and pepper			
Lemon slices, to garnish			

1 Fry (sauté) the vegetables, garlic and curry paste in the oil for 1 minute.

2 Add the stock and tomato purée, bring to the boil and simmer for 5 minutes.

3 Purée in a blender or food processor. Thicken, if liked, with mashed potato and season to taste. Reheat.

4 Serve in warm soup bowls with a lemon slice on top.

PREPARATION TIME: 2 MINUTES

COOKING TIME: 7 MINUTES

STARTERS

A starter should set the taste buds tingling in anticipation of what else is to come, so remember to keep portions small. Many of the following recipes would also make delicious light lunches served with lots of crusty bread and a side salad. And of course they're as easy to make as falling off a log!

Flageolets Vinaigrette sounds delicious doesn't it? Well, simply drain and rinse a can of flageolet beans. Toss with a crushed garlic clove, 45 ml/3 tbsp of olive oil, 15 ml/1 tbsp of white wine vinegar and some thyme, chopped parsley and seasoning and serve with crusty bread.

Artichoke and Prawn
Moscova

SERVES 4	METRIC	IMPERIAL	AMERICAN
Can of artichoke hearts	425 g	15 oz	1 large
Frozen peeled prawns (shrimp), thawed	175 g	6 oz	6 oz
Olive oil	45 ml	3 tbsp	3 tbsp
White wine vinegar	15 ml	1 tbsp	1 tbsp
Salt and pepper			
Soured (dairy sour) cream	150 ml	¼ pt	⅔ cup
Jar of Danish lumpfish roe, to garnish	50 g	2 oz	1 small

1 Drain the artichokes and roughly chop them. Mix with the prawns.

2 Sprinkle over the oil, vinegar and a little salt and pepper and toss lightly.

3 Spoon into four wine goblets. Top each with a spoonful of soured cream. Chill.

4 Just before serving, top the cream with a spoonful of Danish lumpfish roe.

PREPARATION TIME:
5 MINUTES
PLUS CHILLING TIME

Tuna Cheese

Cartons of soft cheese freeze well.

SERVES 4–6	METRIC	IMPERIAL	AMERICAN
Can tuna, drained	185 g	6½ oz	1 small
Low-fat soft cheese	200 g	7 oz	scant 1 cup
Lemon juice	15 ml	1 tbsp	1 tbsp
Cayenne	1.5 ml	¼ tsp	¼ tsp
Salt and pepper			
Chopped parsley	15 ml	1 tbsp	1 tbsp
Paprika, lemon wedges and parsley sprigs or salad leaves, to garnish			
Hot toast, to serve			

1 Mash the tuna in a bowl with the cheese.

2 Add the remaining ingredients and mix well.

3 Either shape into a sausage on greaseproof (waxed) paper and roll up, or pack into four ramekin dishes (custard cups). Chill.

4 Cut the roll into 12 slices. Place the slices or ramekins on individual plates and garnish with paprika, lemon wedges and parsley or salad leaves. Serve with hot toast.

PREPARATION TIME:
5 MINUTES
PLUS CHILLING TIME

Sardine Pâté

SERVES 6	METRIC	IMPERIAL	AMERICAN
Cans of sardines in oil	2×125 g	2×5 oz	2 small
Butter, melted	75 g	3 oz	⅓ cup
Plain yoghurt	150 ml	¼ pt	⅔ cup
Lemon juice	5 ml	1 tsp	1 tsp
Cayenne	1.5 ml	¼ tsp	¼ tsp
Salt and pepper			

Wedges of hard-boiled (hard-cooked) egg,
   small onion rings and chopped parsley, to garnish

Melba toast, to serve

1 Drain the sardines and place in a food processor or blender with the butter, yoghurt, lemon juice and cayenne. Run the machine until smooth.

2 Add salt and pepper to taste, then pack into a small pot and chill for about 2 hours until firm.

3 Spoon on to individual plates. Garnish with wedges of egg, onion rings and chopped parsley. Serve with melba toast.

PREPARATION TIME:
5 MINUTES
PLUS CHILLING TIME

Marinated Kipper Fillets

Make this dish in the morning and it will be ready for dinner.

SERVES 6	METRIC	IMPERIAL	AMERICAN
Packets of frozen kipper fillets, thawed	2×175 g	2×6 oz	2 small
Small onion, separated into rings	1	1	1
Bay leaf	1	1	1
Olive oil	90 ml	6 tbsp	6 tbsp
Red wine vinegar	30 ml	2 tbsp	2 tbsp
Dijon mustard	5 ml	1 tsp	1 tsp
Caster (superfine) sugar	1.5 ml	¼ tsp	¼ tsp
Salt and pepper			
Parsley sprigs, to garnish			
Brown bread and butter, to serve			

1 Pull the skin off the kipper fillets and lay the fish in a large shallow dish. Arrange the onion rings over and add the bay leaf.

2 Whisk together the remaining ingredients and pour over the fish. Leave in a cool place to marinate for several hours, turning occasionally, until the fish feels tender when pierced with the point of a knife.

3 Remove the bay leaf. Fold the fillets and arrange decoratively in shallow individual serving dishes. Spoon the marinade and onion rings over. Garnish with parsley and serve with brown bread and butter.

PREPARATION TIME:
5 MINUTES

MARINATING TIME:
2–3 HOURS

Ham and Pineapple Cocktail

SERVES 6	METRIC	IMPERIAL	AMERICAN
Long-grain rice	75 g	3 oz	⅓ cup
Olive oil	30 ml	2 tbsp	2 tbsp
Lemon juice	10 ml	2 tsp	2 tsp
Soy sauce	5 ml	1 tsp	1 tsp
Small onion, finely chopped	½	½	½
Can of ham	215 g	7½ oz	1 small
Can of pineapple chunks in natural juice	225 g	8 oz	1 small
Black olives, stoned (pitted)	12	12	12
Mayonnaise	30 ml	2 tbsp	2 tbsp

1 Cook the rice in plenty of boiling, salted water for 10 minutes until tender. Drain, rinse with cold water and drain again.

2 Mix together the olive oil, lemon juice, soy sauce and onion. Add to the rice, toss well and divide between six plates, forming a ring of rice on each plate.

3 Dice the ham, discarding any jelly. Drain the pineapple, reserving 15 ml/1 tbsp of the juice.

4 Quarter six of the olives and mix with the ham and pineapple. Pile into the rice rings. Mix the mayonnaise with the reserved pineapple juice and spoon a little over each. Garnish with whole olives.

PREPARATION TIME:
5 MINUTES

COOKING TIME:
10 MINUTES

Corn Fritters with Peanut Sauce

SERVES 4–6	METRIC	IMPERIAL	AMERICAN
Peanut sauce:			
Can of coconut milk	300 g	11 oz	1 small
Crunchy peanut butter	75 ml	5 tbsp	5 tbsp
Caster (superfine) sugar	10 ml	2 tsp	2 tsp
Chilli powder	1.5 ml	¼ tsp	¼ tsp
Lemon juice	5 ml	1 tsp	1 tsp
Garlic clove, crushed	1	1	1
Corn fritters:			
Plain (all-purpose) flour	90 ml	6 tbsp	6 tbsp
Eggs	2	2	2
Milk	60 ml	4 tbsp	4 tbsp
Can of sweetcorn (corn), drained	300 g	11 oz	1 small
Salt and pepper			
Oil for shallow-frying			

1 Put all the sauce ingredients in a pan and heat through gently, stirring occasionally, until boiling.

2 Put the flour in a bowl. Beat the eggs and milk together. Add to the flour and beat until smooth.

3 Add the corn and a little seasoning. Mix well.

4 Heat the oil in a large frying pan (skillet). Fry (sauté) spoonfuls of the corn batter until golden on the base, then turn and fry the other side. Drain well on kitchen paper.

5 Spoon the sauce into individual dishes on serving plates, arrange the fritters around and serve hot.

PREPARATION TIME:
5 MINUTES

COOKING TIME:
10 MINUTES

Mulled Florida Cocktail

SERVES 6	METRIC	IMPERIAL	AMERICAN
Can of mandarin oranges in syrup	300 g	11 oz	1 small
Can of grapefruit segments in syrup	410 g	14½ oz	1 large
White wine	60 ml	4 tbsp	4 tbsp
Cinnamon stick	1	1	1
Cloves	2	2	2
Maraschino cherries, to garnish	6	6	6

1 Drain the syrup from both fruits into a saucepan. Add the wine, cinnamon stick and cloves. Bring to the boil, reduce the heat and simmer very gently for 3 minutes.

2 Remove the cinnamon and cloves, add the fruit and heat through gently but do not boil.

3 Spoon into wine goblets. Top each with a maraschino cherry and serve straight away.

PREPARATION TIME:
2 MINUTES

COOKING TIME:
3 MINUTES

Sicilian Pimientos

	METRIC	IMPERIAL	AMERICAN
SERVES 4–6			
Cans of whole pimientos	2×400 g	2×14 oz	2 large
Olive oil	45 ml	3 tbsp	3 tbsp
Coarse sea salt			
A few black or green olives (optional), to garnish			
Hot ciabatta bread, to serve			

1 Drain the pimientos and dry on kitchen paper.

2 Heat the oil in a large frying pan (skillet) and fry
   (sauté) the pimientos for 1–2 minutes on each side
   until sizzling.

3 Transfer to warm serving plates and drizzle the oil
   from the pan over. Sprinkle with coarse sea salt,
   garnish with olives, if using, and serve straight away
   with hot ciabatta bread.

PREPARATION TIME:
2 MINUTES

COOKING TIME:
2–4 MINUTES

Pears with Blue Cheese Dressing

SERVES 6	METRIC	IMPERIAL	AMERICAN
Can of pear halves, drained	550 g	1 lb 4 oz	1 very large
A few lettuce leaves			
Danish blue cheese	100 g	4 oz	4 oz
Cream, preferably double (heavy)	60 ml	4 tbsp	4 tbsp
Mayonnaise	45 ml	3 tbsp	3 tbsp
Lemon juice	5 ml	1 tsp	1 tsp
A little milk			
Paprika, to garnish			

1 Arrange the pears, rounded sides up, on lettuce leaves on serving plates.

2 Mash the cheese, then beat in half the cream until fairly smooth.

3 Beat in the remaining cream, the mayonnaise and lemon juice. Thin with a little milk, if necessary, to give a coating consistency.

4 Spoon over the pears and garnish with a dusting of paprika.

PREPARATION TIME:
4 MINUTES

Pâté Nests

SERVES 4	METRIC	IMPERIAL	AMERICAN
Slices of bread, from sliced loaf	4	4	4
Butter or margarine for spreading			
Smooth liver pâté	100 g	4 oz	4 oz
Mayonnaise	15 ml	1 tbsp	1 tbsp
Hard-boiled (hard-cooked) egg, finely chopped	1	1	1
Cocktail gherkins (cornichons), finely chopped	4	4	4
Paprika, to garnish			

1 Cut the crusts off the bread and spread the slices liberally with butter or margarine.

2 Press firmly into four sections of a tartlet tin (patty pan).

3 Bake in the oven at 190°C/375°F/gas mark 5 for about 25 minutes or until golden brown. Transfer to a wire rack to cool.

4 Mash the pâté with the mayonnaise. Stir in the chopped egg and gherkins. Pile into the bread cases and dust with paprika.

PREPARATION TIME:
5 MINUTES

COOKING TIME:
25 MINUTES
PLUS COOLING TIME

Melon Cocktail with Herby Cheese Slices

SERVES 4–6	METRIC	IMPERIAL	AMERICAN
Can of melon balls	410 g	14½ oz	1 large
Can of mandarin oranges	300 g	11 oz	1 small
Ginger wine	60 ml	4 tbsp	4 tbsp
Small French stick	1	1	1
Garlic and herb soft cheese	90 g	3½ oz	scant ½ cup
Butter or margarine	25 g	1 oz	2 tbsp

1 Put the contents of the cans of melon and mandarins into a glass bowl. Pour over the ginger wine, stir, then chill until ready to serve.

2 Cut the French stick into 12 slices. Toast on one side under a grill (broiler). Mash together the cheese and butter or margarine and spread over the untoasted sides of the bread.

3 Just before serving, grill (broil) until the cheese mixture is melted and bubbling. Serve straight away with the fruit cocktail.

PREPARATION TIME:
2 MINUTES
PLUS CHILLING TIME

COOKING TIME:
5 MINUTES

Creamy Mussels

SERVES 6	METRIC	IMPERIAL	AMERICAN
Onion, finely chopped	1	1	1
Butter or margarine	15 g	½ oz	1 tbsp
Cans of mussels in brine	2×250 g	2×9 oz	2 small
White wine or dry vermouth	150 ml	¼ pt	⅔ cup
Water	150 ml	¼ pt	⅔ cup
Cornflour (cornstarch)	15 ml	1 tbsp	1 tbsp
Single (light) cream	150 ml	¼ pt	⅔ cup
Pepper			
Chopped parsley	30 ml	2 tbsp	2 tbsp
French bread, to serve			

1 Fry (sauté) the onion in the butter or margarine for 2 minutes until soft but not browned.

2 Drain one of the cans of mussels and add them to the onion with the complete contents of the other can. Add the wine.

3 Blend the water with the cornflour and stir in. Bring to the boil, stirring until thickened.

4 Stir in the cream, pepper to taste and the chopped parsley. Heat through but do not boil. Spoon into bowls and serve with French bread.

PREPARATION TIME:
2 MINUTES

COOKING TIME:
8 MINUTES

Herring and Potato Salad

SERVES 6	METRIC	IMPERIAL	AMERICAN
Rollmop herrings	4	4	4
Can of new potatoes, drained	275 g	10 oz	1 small
Mayonnaise	30 ml	2 tbsp	2 tbsp
Plain yoghurt	15 ml	1 tbsp	1 tbsp
Dried dill (dill weed)	5 ml	1 tsp	1 tsp
Black pepper			
Lettuce leaves and a little extra dill (dill weed), to garnish			
Rye bread, to serve			

1 Using a sharp knife, slice each rollmop into six pin-wheels.

2 Cut the potatoes in quarters or sixths.

3 Mix together the mayonnaise, yoghurt and dill and season with pepper. Add to the potatoes and toss lightly.

4 Put a small pile of potato on to lettuce leaves on each of six serving plates. Arrange four slices of rollmop alongside attractively. Dust the potato with a little more dill. Chill, if time, before serving with rye bread.

PREPARATION TIME:
3 MINUTES
PLUS CHILLING TIME

Tuna Dip

SERVES 4–6	METRIC	IMPERIAL	AMERICAN
Can of tuna, drained	185 g	6½ oz	1 small
Mayonnaise	60 ml	4 tbsp	4 tbsp
Plain yoghurt	45 ml	3 tbsp	3 tbsp
Tomato ketchup (catsup)	15 ml	1 tbsp	1 tbsp
Lemon juice	5 ml	1 tsp	1 tsp
Chilli powder	1.5 ml	¼ tsp	¼ tsp
Pepper			
Vegetable 'dippers' or plain crisps (potato chips) or crisp toast fingers, to serve			

1 Put the tuna in a bowl and break up with a wooden spoon.

2 Beat in the remaining ingredients until well blended. Turn into a small bowl and surround with vegetable 'dippers' such as small cauliflower florets, cucumber, carrot and green and red (bell) pepper sticks, or crisps, or crisp toast fingers.

PREPARATION TIME:
3 MINUTES
PLUS CHILLING TIME

Middle Eastern Dip

Use other pulses such as canned butter beans, flageolet or cannellini beans if you prefer.

SERVES 4–6	METRIC	IMPERIAL	AMERICAN
Can of chick peas (garbanzos), drained	440 g	15½ oz	1 large
Garlic clove, crushed	1	1	1
Olive oil	90 ml	6 tbsp	6 tbsp
Lemon juice	15 ml	1 tbsp	1 tbsp
Salt and pepper			
A little olive oil			
Dried mint, to garnish			
Warm pitta bread fingers, to serve			

1 Put the chick peas and garlic in a blender or food processor and run the machine until they are smooth.

2 Gradually add the oil in a thin stream while the machine is running.

3 Add the lemon juice and season with salt and pepper.

4 Turn into a small bowl, drizzle a little olive oil over and sprinkle with dried mint. Serve with warm pitta bread fingers.

PREPARATION TIME:
4 MINUTES

Nutty Cheese and Pineapple

This mixture can also be used to top pear or peach halves.

SERVES 4	METRIC	IMPERIAL	AMERICAN
Can of pineapple slices, drained	225 g	8 oz	1 small
A few lettuce leaves			
Cottage cheese	225 g	8 oz	1 cup
Walnut pieces, chopped	50 g	2 oz	½ cup
Grated onion	2.5 ml	½ tsp	½ tsp
Black pepper			
Paprika, to garnish			
Garlic bread (see Garlic Butter page 157), to serve			

1 Dry the pineapple slices on kitchen paper. Arrange on lettuce leaves on four individual plates.

2 Mix together the cheese, nuts and onion and season with a little pepper.

3 Pile the mixture into the centres of the pineapple rings so you can still see a rim of pineapple. Dust with paprika and chill, if time allows, before serving with garlic bread.

PREPARATION TIME:
3 MINUTES
PLUS CHILLING TIME

FISH

Many people are turning to fish as it is light, easily digestible and suitable for all but vegans. With so many canned and frozen varieties available, it makes the ideal choice for a quick meal. Here's Spicy Cod with Beans to set off your imagination. To 4 lightly fried (sautéed) cod steaks, add a small can of chopped tomatoes, a small can of drained green beans, 15 ml/ 1 tbsp of tomato purée (paste), 5 ml/1 tsp of caster (superfine) sugar and a pinch of cayenne. Heat through for 6 minutes, then serve on a bed of rice.

Cheesy Prawn Supper

SERVES 4	METRIC	IMPERIAL	AMERICAN
Frozen peeled prawns (shrimp), thawed	225 g	8 oz	8 oz
Can of condensed cream of mushroom soup	295 g	10½ oz	1 small
Tomato ketchup (catsup)	15 ml	1 tbsp	1 tbsp
Fresh breadcrumbs	50 g	2 oz	1 cup
Cheddar cheese, grated	100 g	4 oz	1 cup
Plain boiled rice, toasted flaked (slivered) almonds and broccoli, to serve			

1 Mix the prawns with the soup, ketchup and half the breadcrumbs and cheese.

2 Turn into a fairly shallow ovenproof serving dish.

3 Mix together the remaining breadcrumbs and cheese and spoon over.

4 Bake in the oven at 200°C/400°F/gas mark 6 for 20–25 minutes until golden and bubbling.

5 Garnish with toasted almonds and serve with boiled rice and broccoli.

PREPARATION TIME: 3 MINUTES

COOKING TIME: 20–25 MINUTES

Smoked Mackerel Bake

SERVES 4	METRIC	IMPERIAL	AMERICAN
Frozen or canned smoked mackerel fillets	4	4	4
Can of button mushrooms, drained	300 g	11 oz	1 small
Packet of white sauce mix	1	1	1
Milk or water, according to packet directions			
Horseradish cream	20 ml	4 tsp	4 tsp
Cheese and onion crisps (potato chips), crushed	50 g	2 oz	2 oz
New potatoes and peas, to serve			

1 Remove the skin from the fillets, break the fish into pieces and place in a fairly shallow ovenproof dish. Scatter the mushrooms over.

2 Make up the sauce according to the packet directions and blend in the horseradish.

3 Pour the sauce over the fish and sprinkle with the crushed crisps. Bake in the oven at 190°C/375°F/gas mark 5 for about 30 minutes or until bubbling and golden. Serve with new potatoes and peas.

PREPARATION TIME:
3 MINUTES

COOKING TIME:
30 MINUTES

Tuna Gnocchi

SERVES 4	METRIC	IMPERIAL	AMERICAN
Milk	600 ml	1 pt	2½ cups
Salt	7.5 ml	1½ tsp	1½ tsp
Pepper			
Bay leaf	1	1	1
Grated nutmeg	1.5 ml	¼ tsp	¼ tsp
Semolina (cream of wheat)	150 g	5 oz	scant 1 cup
Eggs	2	2	2
Cheddar cheese, grated	100 g	4 oz	1 cup
Can of tuna, drained	185 g	6½ oz	1 small
Can of condensed cream of mushroom soup	295 g	10½ oz	1 small
Melted butter for brushing			

1 Put the milk, salt, a little pepper, the bay leaf, nutmeg and semolina in a pan. Bring to the boil and cook for 10 minutes, stirring until really thick. Discard the bay leaf.

2 Beat in the eggs and 75 g/3 oz/¾ cup of the cheese. Turn into a well-greased baking tin (pan) and smooth out with a wet palette knife to a square about 2 cm/¾ in thick. Leave to cool, then chill for 1 hour.

3 Meanwhile, mix the tuna with the soup. Turn into a 1.2 litre/2 pt/5 cup ovenproof dish. Cut the gnocchi into 4 cm/1½ in squares and arrange around the top of the dish. Brush with a little melted butter and sprinkle with the remaining cheese.

4 Bake in the oven at 200°C/400°F/gas mark 6 for 30 minutes until golden.

PREPARATION TIME:
15 MINUTES
PLUS CHILLING TIME

COOKING TIME:
30 MINUTES

Seaside Crumble

SERVES 4	METRIC	IMPERIAL	AMERICAN
Plain (all-purpose) flour	75 g	3 oz	¾ cup
Butter or margarine, softened	40 g	1½ oz	3 tbsp
Cheddar cheese, grated	50 g	2 oz	½ cup
Frozen white fish fillets, thawed	450 g	1 lb	1 lb
Can of condensed celery soup	295 g	10½ oz	1 small
Frozen mixed vegetables	100 g	4 oz	4 oz
Chopped parsley	15 ml	1 tbsp	1 tbsp

1 Work the butter or margarine into the flour with a fork until crumbly. Stir in the cheese.

2 Dice the fish, discarding any skin and bones.

3 Place in an ovenproof serving dish and mix in the soup, vegetables and parsley.

4 Spoon the crumble over and bake in the oven at 200°C/400°F/gas mark 6 for about 30 minutes until golden brown and cooked through.

PREPARATION TIME:
5 MINUTES

COOKING TIME:
30 MINUTES

Tuna and Corn Pasta

SERVES 4	METRIC	IMPERIAL	AMERICAN
Pasta shapes	225 g	8 oz	8 oz
Packet of cheese sauce mix	1	1	1
Milk or water, according to packet directions			
Can of tuna, drained	185 g	6½ oz	1 small
Can of sweetcorn (corn), drained	200 g	7 oz	1 small
A little Cheddar cheese, grated (optional)			
Chopped parsley, to garnish			
Salad, to serve			

1 Cook the pasta according to the packet directions. Drain.

2 Meanwhile, make up the cheese sauce with milk or water according to the packet directions. Add the tuna and sweetcorn, stir and heat through.

3 Add to the drained pasta and toss well. Either serve as it is, sprinkled with chopped parsley, or turn into a flameproof serving dish, top with a little grated cheese and brown under a hot grill (broiler) before garnishing and serving with salad.

PREPARATION TIME: 2 MINUTES

COOKING TIME: 10–12 MINUTES

Jansen's Quick Temptation

This recipe is based on the famous potato dish.

SERVES 4	METRIC	IMPERIAL	AMERICAN
Cans of new potatoes	2×275 g	2×10 oz	2 small
Garlic clove, crushed	1	1	1
Can of anchovies	50 g	2 oz	1 small
Butter, melted	75 g	3 oz	⅓ cup
Single (light) cream	150 ml	¼ pt	⅔ cup
Fresh breadcrumbs	50 g	2 oz	1 cup
Cheddar cheese, grated	50 g	2 oz	½ cup
Grated carrot and cucumber salad, to serve			

1 Drain and slice the potatoes. Mix with the garlic and the oil from the anchovies. Chop the fish and add to the mixture.

2 Grease an ovenproof serving dish with some of the butter. Tip in the potato mixture and level the surface. Pour the cream over.

3 Mix the remaining butter with the breadcrumbs and cheese and sprinkle on top.

4 Bake at 200°C/400°F/gas mark 6 for about 35 minutes or until golden. Serve hot with a grated carrot and cucumber salad.

PREPARATION TIME:
5 MINUTES

COOKING TIME:
35 MINUTES

Salmon in Filo Pastry

SERVES 4–6

	METRIC	IMPERIAL	AMERICAN
Can of red salmon	425 g	15 oz	1 large
Filo pastry (paste) sheets	4–6	4–6	4–6
Butter, melted	50 g	2 oz	¼ cup
Can of creamed mushrooms	215 g	7½ oz	1 small
Pinch of dried basil or dill (dill weed)			
Passata (sieved tomatoes)	60–90 ml	4–6 tbsp	4–6 tbsp
Lemon wedges and parsley sprigs (optional), to garnish			
New potatoes and green salad, to serve			

1 Drain the salmon and carefully remove the central backbone and any skin.

2 Lay a sheet of filo pastry on a board (keep the remainder wrapped). Brush lightly with melted butter. Fold in half and brush lightly again. Note: if the sheets are small squares instead of larger rectangles, brush one with butter and top with a second sheet instead of folding (you will therefore need 8–12 sheets).

3 Place a spoonful of mushrooms in the centre of the pastry. Top with a quarter or sixth of the salmon and sprinkle with a good pinch of basil or dill.

4 Draw up the edges over the filling and pinch together to form a pouch. Transfer to a buttered baking sheet.

5 Repeat with the remaining ingredients. Brush all the parcels with a little more butter and bake in the oven at 200°C/400°F/gas mark 6 for about 10–15 minutes until golden brown.

6 Meanwhile, heat the passata. When ready to serve, put the parcels on to warm serving plates. Put a spoonful of passata to one side of each parcel and garnish with a lemon wedge and a parsley sprig, if using. Serve with new potatoes and a green salad.

PREPARATION TIME:
10 MINUTES

COOKING TIME:
10–15 MINUTES

Quick Party Paella

SERVES 4	METRIC	IMPERIAL	AMERICAN
Packet of savoury mushroom or vegetable rice	1	1	1
Boiling water	450 ml	¾ pt	2 cups
Cooked chicken, diced	100 g	4 oz	1 cup
Can of mussels, drained	250 g	9 oz	1 small
Frozen peeled prawns (shrimp)	100 g	4 oz	4 oz
Crusty bread and salad, to serve			

1 Put the rice in a pan with the boiling water. Stir, cover and simmer for 12 minutes.

2 Add the remaining ingredients, stir, cover and simmer gently for a further 8 minutes until all the liquid has been absorbed and the rice is tender. Serve with crusty bread and salad.

PREPARATION TIME:
4 MINUTES

COOKING TIME:
20 MINUTES

Salmon Flan

Freeze the rest of the pimiento caps and anchovies for use later.

SERVES 4	METRIC	IMPERIAL	AMERICAN
Shortcrust pastry (basic pie crust)	175 g	6 oz	6 oz
Packet of white sauce mix	1	1	1
Milk or water, according to packet directions			
Can of salmon	185 g	6½ oz	1 small
Tomato purée (paste)	15 ml	1 tbsp	1 tbsp
Canned pimiento cap, chopped	1	1	1
Canned anchovy fillets	5	5	5
Stuffed olives, halved	3	3	3
Crusty bread and salad, to serve			

1 Roll out the pastry and use to line an 18 cm/7 in flan dish (pie pan). Prick the base with a fork, then line with crumpled foil and bake at 200°C/400°F/gas mark 6 for 10 minutes. Remove the foil and bake for a further 5 minutes until golden brown.

2 Meanwhile, make up the white sauce according to the packet directions. Flake the fish, discarding any bones and skin and add to the sauce with the tomato purée and pimiento.

3 If serving hot, reheat.

4 Turn into the pastry case (shell), decorate with the anchovies and olives and serve hot. Alternatively, leave until cold before serving with bread and salad.

PREPARATION TIME:
5 MINUTES

COOKING TIME:
15 MINUTES
PLUS COOLING TIME

Saucy Cod Puffs

SERVES 4	METRIC	IMPERIAL	AMERICAN
Frozen puff pastry (paste), just thawed	350 g	12 oz	12 oz
Tomatoes, chopped (optional)	2	2	2
Frozen cod steaks in parsley sauce	4	4	4
Beaten egg, to glaze	1	1	1
Creamed potatoes and green beans, to serve			

1 Cut the pastry into quarters. Roll out and trim each to about 18 cm/7 in square.

2 If using tomatoes, divide between the four pastry pieces.

3 Carefully remove the fish and sauce from the bag and place on top of the tomato.

4 Brush the edges of the pastry with beaten egg and fold over the fish to form parcels. Press the edges well together to seal.

5 Transfer the parcels, sealed sides down, to a dampened baking sheet. Brush with beaten egg. Make 'leaves' out of any pastry trimmings, place on the parcels and brush with a little more egg.

6 Bake at 220°C/425°F/gas mark 7 for 15–20 minutes until puffy, golden and cooked through. Serve hot with creamed potatoes and green beans.

PREPARATION TIME:
10 MINUTES

COOKING TIME:
15–20 MINUTES

Fisherman's Pizza

SERVES 2–4	METRIC	IMPERIAL	AMERICAN
Pizza base (ready-made)	23 cm	9 in	9 in
Tomato purée (paste)	45 ml	3 tbsp	3 tbsp
Packet of cheese sauce mix	1	1	1
Milk or water, according to packet directions, but a little less than recommended			
Can of sild (or small sardines) in oil, drained	120 g	4½ oz	1 small
Cheddar cheese, grated	50 g	2 oz	½ cup
Chopped parsley, to garnish			
Jacket potatoes and tomato and onion salad, to serve			

1 Put the pizza base on a baking sheet.

2 Spread with the tomato purée to within 1 cm/½ in of the edge.

3 Make up the cheese sauce using less than the recommended amount of milk or water (to give a thicker consistency).

4 Spread over the tomato purée. Arrange the fish in a starburst pattern on top and sprinkle with the grated cheese.

5 Bake in the oven at 220°C/425°F/gas mark 7 for about 20 minutes or until golden and bubbling. Serve hot with jacket potatoes and tomato and onion salad.

PREPARATION TIME:
5 MINUTES

COOKING TIME:
20 MINUTES

Fish Mousse

SERVES 6–8	METRIC	IMPERIAL	AMERICAN
Can of tuna or salmon	425 g	15 oz	1 large
Sachet of powdered gelatine	1	1	1
Water	30 ml	2 tbsp	2 tbsp
Mayonnaise	45 ml	3 tbsp	3 tbsp
Tomato purée (paste)	15 ml	1 tbsp	1 tbsp
Anchovy essence (extract) (optional)	10 ml	2 tsp	2 tsp
Lemon juice	30 ml	2 tbsp	2 tbsp
Salt and pepper			
Double (heavy) or whipping cream	300 ml	½ pt	1¼ cups
Mixed salad, to serve			

1 Drain the fish and mash well, discarding any skin and bones.

2 Dissolve the gelatine in the water according to the packet directions.

3 Add the mayonnaise, tomato purée, anchovy essence, if using, lemon juice and a little salt and pepper to the fish and beat well. Beat in the dissolved gelatine.

4 Whip the cream until softly peaking and fold into the fish mixture with a metal spoon. Turn into an oiled mould or serving dish. Chill until set.

5 Just before serving, turn out, if necessary, on to a serving plate and serve with a mixed salad.

PREPARATION TIME:
10 MINUTES
PLUS SETTING TIME

Peppered Trout

SERVES 4	METRIC	IMPERIAL	AMERICAN
Frozen rainbow trout, just thawed	4	4	4
Oil	15 ml	1 tbsp	1 tbsp
Butter or margarine	15 g	½ oz	1 tbsp
Soft cheese with black pepper	90 g	3½ oz	scant ½ cup
Milk	45 ml	3 tbsp	3 tbsp
Chopped parsley, to garnish			
Sautéed potatoes and broccoli, to serve			

1 Rinse the fish, dry on kitchen paper and cut off the heads, if preferred.

2 Heat the oil and butter or margarine in a large frying pan (skillet) and fry (sauté) the fish for 5 minutes on each side until cooked through. Transfer to a warm serving plate and keep warm.

3 Strain the cooking juices into a saucepan (to avoid any bits of skin in the sauce). Add the cheese and 30 ml/2 tbsp of the milk. Heat through gently, stirring, until the cheese melts. Add a little more milk until the sauce is of a pouring consistency.

4 Pour the sauce over the fish, sprinkle with chopped parsley and serve with sautéed potatoes and broccoli.

PREPARATION TIME: 4 MINUTES

COOKING TIME: 12 MINUTES

Crab Thermidor

SERVES 4	METRIC	IMPERIAL	AMERICAN
Packet of white sauce mix	1	1	1
Milk or water, according to packet directions, but a little less than recommended			
Brandy	15 ml	1 tbsp	1 tbsp
Dijon mustard	5 ml	1 tsp	1 tsp
Dried mixed herbs	2.5 ml	½ tsp	½ tsp
Cans of white crabmeat	2×175 g	2×6 oz	2 small
Fresh breadcrumbs	50 g	2 oz	1 cup
Butter or margarine, melted	25 g	1 oz	2 tbsp
Cheddar cheese, grated	50 g	2 oz	½ cup
Chopped parsley, to garnish			
New potatoes and crisp green salad, to serve			

1 Make up the sauce using slightly less than the recommended amount of liquid. Stir in the brandy, mustard and herbs.

2 Spoon a layer of half the sauce into the base of four individual gratin or other shallow flameproof dishes.

3 Top with the drained crabmeat, then cover with the rest of the sauce.

4 Mix together the breadcrumbs, butter or margarine and grated cheese. Sprinkle over. Place under a moderate grill (broiler) for about 5–8 minutes until golden brown and hot. Garnish with parsley and serve with new potatoes and a green salad.

PREPARATION TIME:
5 MINUTES

COOKING TIME:
8–10 MINUTES

Quick Fish Pot

SERVES 4	METRIC	IMPERIAL	AMERICAN
Frozen white fish fillet	350 g	12 oz	12 oz
Can of chopped tomatoes	400 g	14 oz	1 large
Vegetable or fish stock	300 ml	½ pt	1¼ cups
Anchovy essence (extract)	5 ml	1 tsp	1 tsp
Can of new potatoes, drained and quartered	275 g	10 oz	1 small
Can of sliced carrots, drained	275 g	10 oz	1 small
Can of garden peas, drained	275 g	10 oz	1 small
Salt and pepper			
Chopped parsley, to garnish			
Crusty bread, to serve			

1 Cut the fish into small chunks, discarding the skin and any bones.

2 Place the tomatoes and stock in a large saucepan. Add the remaining ingredients, adding the fish last.

3 Bring to the boil, reduce the heat, cover and simmer for 5 minutes until the fish is tender. Stir gently and season to taste. Ladle into large, warm soup bowls, garnish with parsley and serve with lots of crusty bread.

PREPARATION TIME: 3 MINUTES

COOKING TIME: 5 MINUTES

Smoked Haddock Florentine

Use white fish if you prefer.

SERVES 4	METRIC	IMPERIAL	AMERICAN
Frozen chopped spinach	450 g	1 lb	1 lb
Packets of boil-in-the-bag smoked haddock	2×175 g	2×6 oz	2 small
Packet of cheese sauce mix	1	1	1
Milk or water, according to packet directions			
A little grated Cheddar cheese (optional)			
Poached eggs (optional), crisp toast triangles and canned or stewed fresh tomatoes, to serve			

1 Cook the spinach according to the packet directions. Drain and spread in the base of a 1.2 litre/2 pt/5 cup flameproof dish.

2 Cook the fish according to the packet directions. Lay on top of the spinach.

3 Make up the sauce according to the packet directions. Spoon over the fish. Cover with grated cheese, if using.

4 Place under a hot grill (broiler) until golden and bubbling. Serve with poached eggs, if liked, toast triangles and canned or stewed fresh tomatoes.

PREPARATION TIME: 3 MINUTES

COOKING TIME: 10 MINUTES

Spaghetti with Clams

SERVES 4	METRIC	IMPERIAL	AMERICAN
Spaghetti	350 g	12 oz	12 oz
Onion, chopped	1	1	1
Garlic clove, crushed	1	1	1
Olive oil	15 ml	1 tbsp	1 tbsp
Passata (sieved tomatoes)	300 ml	½ pt	1¼ cups
Can of baby clams, drained	300 g	11 oz	1 small
Salt and black pepper			
Chopped parsley, to garnish			
Green salad, to serve			

1 Cook the spaghetti in plenty of boiling, salted water for 10 minutes or until just tender. Drain.

2 Meanwhile, fry (sauté) the onion and garlic in the oil for 3 minutes, stirring, until softened but not browned. Add the passata, clams and a little salt and pepper and simmer for 5 minutes.

3 Add to the spaghetti and toss well. Garnish with chopped parsley and serve with a green salad.

PREPARATION TIME:
3 MINUTES

COOKING TIME:
10 MINUTES

Smoky Jackets

SERVES 4	METRIC	IMPERIAL	AMERICAN
Potatoes, scrubbed	4 large	4 large	4 large
Butter or margarine	25 g	1 oz	2 tbsp
Low-fat soft cheese	225 g	8 oz	1 cup
Can of smoked mussels	100 g	4 oz	1 small
Snipped chives or chopped parsley	15 ml	1 tbsp	1 tbsp
A little lemon juice			
Salt and pepper			
Mixed salad, to serve			

1 Make a cut lengthwise round the centre of each potato, ready to cut into halves when cooked.

2 Boil in water for about 20 minutes or until tender. (Alternatively, bake in a moderate oven for about 1 hour or microwave or pressure cook according to appliance instructions.)

3 Halve the potatoes and scoop out most of the flesh into a bowl, leaving a 'shell' of skin and potato. Mash the flesh with the butter or margarine and cheese.

4 Drain the mussels and roughly chop or leave whole as preferred. Mix with the potato, add the herbs, a little lemon juice and salt and pepper to taste.

5 Pile the mixture back into the shells and place under a moderate grill (broiler) for about 5 minutes or until golden and hot through. Serve with a mixed salad.

PREPARATION TIME:
8 MINUTES

COOKING TIME:
ABOUT 30 MINUTES

Madame Bovary's Omelette

SERVES 4	METRIC	IMPERIAL	AMERICAN
Small onion, finely chopped	1	1	1
Butter	150 g	5 oz	⅔ cup
Cans of soft cod roes, drained	2 × 100 g	2 × 4 oz	2 small
Can of tuna, drained	85 g	3½ oz	1 small
Eggs, beaten	8	8	8
Salt and pepper			
Chopped parsley	15 ml	1 tbsp	1 tbsp
Dried mixed herbs	5 ml	1 tsp	1 tsp
A little lemon juice			
French bread, to serve			

1 Fry (sauté) the onion in 50 g/2 oz/¼ cup of the butter for about 3 minutes, until softened but not browned.

2 Mix the roes and tuna with the onion. Stir into the beaten eggs and season.

3 Melt 10 g/¼ oz/½ tbsp of the remaining butter in an omelette pan and add a quarter of the mixture. Lift and stir the egg gently in the pan until just set and golden underneath. Fold into three and slide on to a warm serving plate. Keep warm while you make three more omelettes.

4 Melt the remaining butter and stir in the parsley, herbs and a little lemon juice to taste. Pour a little around each omelette and serve with French bread.

PREPARATION TIME:
5 MINUTES

COOKING TIME:
15 MINUTES

Crab and Cheese Tart

SERVES 4	METRIC	IMPERIAL	AMERICAN
Butter, melted	50 g	2 oz	¼ cup
Filo pastry (paste) sheets	8	8	8
Can of crabmeat, drained	175 g	6 oz	1 small
Port Salut or St Paulin cheese	175 g	6 oz	6 oz
Eggs	3	3	3
Crème fraîche or single (light) cream	300 ml	½ pt	1¼ cups
Salt and pepper			
Dried thyme	2.5 ml	½ tsp	½ tsp
Green salad, to serve			

1 Lightly butter a 20 cm/8 in flan tin (pie pan). Layer sheets of pastry in the tin, brushing with butter between layers, allowing the edges of the pastry to hang over the sides of tin.

2 Spread the crabmeat on the pastry base.

3 Cut the orange rind off the cheese and discard. Slice the cheese and lay over the crab.

4 Beat the eggs with the crème fraîche, a little salt and pepper and the thyme. Pour over the filling, then gently fold the pastry flaps over the top. Brush the top lightly with butter.

5 Bake in the oven at 180°C/350°F/gas mark 4 for about 30–35 minutes or until set and golden. Serve warm with a green salad.

PREPARATION TIME:
5 MINUTES

COOKING TIME:
30–35 MINUTES

MEAT AND POULTRY

All the following recipes are filling, tasty and
meaty enough for even the hungriest appetite.
Sometimes all you need is a little
imagination stirred into your favourite
recipes: such as adding a spoonful of herbs to
your toad in the hole batter and serving it
with a packet of onion sauce.

You can do interesting things with leftovers
from your roasts too. Dice cooked chicken and
mix it with enough mayonnaise to coat,
flavoured with a little curry powder and
mango chutney. Try your Curried Chicken
Mayonnaise with a packet of savoury rice,
cooked and cooled – delicious.

Beef in Wine

SERVES 4–6	METRIC	IMPERIAL	AMERICAN
Onion, finely chopped	1	1	1
Oil	15 ml	1 tbsp	1 tbsp
Cans of stewed steak without gravy	2×430 g	2×15 oz	2 large
Red wine	300 ml	½ pt	1¼ cups
Can of button mushrooms	300 g	11 oz	1 small
Can of sliced carrots, drained	275 g	10 oz	1 small
Dried mixed herbs	2.5 ml	½ tsp	½ tsp
Pinch of caster (superfine) sugar			
Cornflour (cornstarch)	20 ml	4 tsp	4 tsp
Salt and pepper			
Creamed potatoes and broccoli, to serve			

1 Fry (sauté) the onion in the oil for 3 minutes until softened but not browned.

2 Add the steak and wine and heat through, stirring to break up the meat.

3 Drain the mushrooms, reserving 30 ml/2 tbsp of the liquid.

4 Add the mushrooms, carrots, herbs and sugar to the pan and continue to heat gently until bubbling.

5 Blend the cornflour with the reserved mushroom liquid. Stir gently into the pan and cook until thickened. Taste and season if necessary. Serve with creamed potatoes and broccoli.

PREPARATION TIME:
5 MINUTES

COOKING TIME:
10 MINUTES

International Beef Pot

SERVES 4–6	METRIC	IMPERIAL	AMERICAN
Cans of stewed steak with or without gravy	2×430 g	2×15 oz	2 large
Can of water chestnuts, drained	225 g	8 oz	1 small
Can of condensed mushroom soup	295 g	10½ oz	1 small
Potatoes, thinly sliced	450 g	1 lb	1 lb
Parsley, to garnish			
A green vegetable, to serve			

1 Empty the meat into a large shallow ovenproof dish and break up with a wooden spoon.

2 Slice the water chestnuts and scatter over.

3 Spoon over half the can of soup.

4 Arrange the potato slices neatly in a single layer over the top.

5 Thin the remaining soup slightly with water and spoon over.

6 Bake in the oven at 200°C/400°F/gas mark 6 for about 45 minutes until the potatoes are cooked and top is golden brown. Garnish with parsley and serve with a green vegetable.

PREPARATION TIME:
5 MINUTES

COOKING TIME:
45 MINUTES

Beef in Beer

SERVES 4–6	METRIC	IMPERIAL	AMERICAN
Cans of stewed steak in gravy	2×430 g	2×15 oz	2 large
Beer	60 ml	4 tbsp	4 tbsp
Brandy	15 ml	1 tbsp	1 tbsp
Instant mashed potato	30 ml	2 tbsp	2 tbsp
Slices of French bread	6–8	6–8	6–8
Butter	25 g	1 oz	2 tbsp
Wholegrain mustard	15 ml	1 tbsp	1 tbsp
Boiled potatoes and green beans, to serve			

1 Empty the cans of meat into a flameproof casserole (Dutch oven) with the beer and brandy. Stir well. Heat through until bubbling.

2 Sprinkle the instant mashed potato over and stir in to thicken.

3 Meanwhile, toast the slices of French bread on one side. Mash together the butter and mustard and spread on the untoasted sides.

4 Arrange, buttered side up, around the top of the casserole. Place under a hot grill (broiler) until toasted and bubbling. Serve hot with boiled potatoes and green beans.

PREPARATION TIME: 5 MINUTES

COOKING TIME: 10 MINUTES

Note: All the following minced (ground) beef recipes can be made with 225 g/8 oz/2 cups frozen meat instead of a can. Dry-fry (sauté) the meat with a chopped onion, then add 300 ml/2 pt/1¼ cups beef stock and simmer for 10 minutes. Thicken with 15 ml/ 1 tbsp cornflour (cornstarch) blended with a little water and add a few drops of gravy browning and seasoning to taste. Then continue as described in the recipes.

Pasta Grill

SERVES 4	METRIC	IMPERIAL	AMERICAN
Pasta shapes	225 g	8 oz	8 oz
Can of minced (ground) steak with onions	425 g	15 oz	1 large
Dried mixed herbs	5 ml	1 tsp	1 tsp
Cheddar cheese, grated	50 g	2 oz	½ cup
Tomatoes, sliced (optional)	2–3	2–3	2–3
Salad, to serve			

1 Cook the pasta according to the packet directions. Drain, rinse with hot water and drain again.

2 Return to the saucepan, add the contents of the can of mince and season with the herbs.

3 Heat through, stirring gently, until piping hot.

4 Turn into a flameproof dish, sprinkle with cheese and arrange the tomato slices around the edge, if using.

5 Brown under a hot grill (broiler) for about 3 minutes, then serve hot with salad.

PREPARATION TIME: 2 MINUTES COOKING TIME: ABOUT 15 MINUTES

Quick Mexican Meal

For less fire, use half the amount of chilli powder.

SERVES 4	METRIC	IMPERIAL	AMERICAN
Can of minced (ground) steak with onions	425 g	15 oz	1 large
Tomato purée (paste)	15 ml	1 tbsp	1 tbsp
Chilli powder	2.5 ml	½ tsp	½ tsp
Garlic clove, crushed	1	1	1
Can of red kidney beans, drained	425 g	15 oz	1 large
Taco shells	12	12	12
Shredded lettuce, chopped tomato, soured (dairy sour) cream and grated Cheddar cheese, to serve			

1 Put the mince in a pan with the tomato purée, chilli powder, garlic and beans. Heat through, stirring, until bubbling.

2 Warm the taco shells in a hot oven or the microwave according to the packet directions. Spoon the chilli mixture into the shells and serve with lettuce, tomato and soured cream and cheese to spoon on top of the meat.

PREPARATION TIME:
5 MINUTES

COOKING TIME:
5 MINUTES

Town House Pie

SERVES 4	METRIC	IMPERIAL	AMERICAN
Can of minced (ground) steak with onions	425 g	15 oz	1 large
Can of baked beans in tomato sauce	225 g	8 oz	1 small
Worcestershire sauce	10 ml	2 tsp	2 tsp
Dried thyme	2.5 ml	½ tsp	½ tsp
Instant mashed potato servings	4	4	4
Cheddar cheese, grated	50 g	2 oz	½ cup
Crusty bread and a green vegetable, to serve			

1 Put the meat, beans, Worcestershire sauce and thyme in a saucepan and heat through until piping hot, stirring occasionally. Turn into a flameproof dish (or put in a dish and heat in the microwave).

2 Meanwhile, make up the potato according to the packet directions. Pile on top of the meat mixture and sprinkle with the cheese.

3 Place under a hot grill (broiler) until golden and bubbling. Serve with crusty bread and a green vegetable.

PREPARATION TIME:
5 MINUTES

COOKING TIME:
ABOUT 5 MINUTES

Savoury Strudel

SERVES 4	METRIC	IMPERIAL	AMERICAN
Filo pastry (paste) sheets	4	4	4
Butter, melted	25 g	1 oz	2 tbsp
Can of minced (ground) steak with onions	425 g	15 oz	1 large
Pinch of grated nutmeg			
Passata (sieved tomatoes)	90 ml	6 tbsp	6 tbsp
Sweetcorn (corn), to serve			

1 Brush a sheet of pastry lightly with butter and lay another sheet on top. Continue layering in this way.

2 Gently spread the meat mixture over the pastry to within 1 cm/½ in of the edge all round.

3 Sprinkle with a little grated nutmeg.

4 Fold in the short sides of the pastry, then roll up from a long end.

5 Carefully transfer the strudel to a lightly buttered baking sheet and shape it into a curve. Brush with a little more butter.

6 Bake in the oven at 200°C/400°F/gas mark 6 for about 20 minutes or until crisp and golden brown. Carefully transfer to a warm serving platter. Heat the passata and spoon around. Serve hot with sweetcorn.

PREPARATION TIME: 5 MINUTES

COOKING TIME: ABOUT 20 MINUTES

Potato Moussaka

SERVES 4	METRIC	IMPERIAL	AMERICAN
Potatoes, scrubbed and sliced (not peeled), or a large can	450 g	1 lb	1 lb
Can of minced (ground) steak with onions	425 g	15 oz	1 large
Garlic clove, crushed	1	1	1
Tomato purée (paste)	15 ml	1 tbsp	1 tbsp
Ground cinnamon	5 ml	1 tsp	1 tsp
Plain yoghurt or single (light) cream	150 ml	¼ pt	⅔ cup
Egg	1	1	1
Salt and pepper			
Cheddar cheese, grated	50 g	2 oz	½ cup
Salad, to serve			

1 Boil the potatoes in salted water for about 5 minutes until tender, then drain. If using canned potatoes, drain and slice them.

2 Mix the mince with the garlic, tomato purée and cinnamon. Layer the potatoes and meat mixture in an ovenproof serving dish, finishing with a layer of potatoes.

3 Beat the yoghurt or cream with the egg and a little salt and pepper. Stir in the cheese. Pour over the potatoes.

4 Bake in the oven at 190°C/375°F/gas mark 5 for about 35 minutes until bubbling, golden and the top has set. Alternatively, cook in a microwave and brown under the grill (broiler).

5 Serve with salad.

PREPARATION TIME:
5 MINUTES

COOKING TIME:
ABOUT 35 MINUTES

Pan Hash

SERVES 4	METRIC	IMPERIAL	AMERICAN
Onions, chopped	2	2	2
Oil	30 ml	2 tbsp	2 tbsp
Cooked potatoes, diced	450 g	1 lb	1 lb
Can of corned beef, diced	350 g	12 oz	1 large
Can of baked beans in tomato sauce	400 g	14 oz	1 large
Brown table sauce	15 ml	1 tbsp	1 tbsp
Salt and pepper			
Crusty bread and salad, to serve			

1 Fry (sauté) the onions in the oil for 3 minutes until softened but not browned.

2 Mix together the remaining ingredients. Add to the pan and fry for 5 minutes, turning occasionally.

3 Press down with a fish slice and fry for a further 5 minutes, without disturbing, until crisp and brown underneath. Serve with crusty bread and salad.

PREPARATION TIME:
5 MINUTES

COOKING TIME:
ABOUT 13 MINUTES

Corned-ish Pasties

SERVES 4	METRIC	IMPERIAL	AMERICAN
Shortcrust pastry (basic pie crust)	350 g	12 oz	12 oz
Can of corned beef, finely diced	185 g	6½ oz	1 small
Can of mixed vegetables, drained	275 g	10 oz	1 small
Pepper			
Egg, beaten	1	1	1
Coleslaw and green salad, to serve			

1 Cut the pastry into quarters and roll out each one to an 18–20 cm/7–8 in circle, using a plate or saucepan lid as a guide.

2 Place equal amounts of the meat and the vegetables in the centre of each pastry circle. Season with pepper. Brush the edges with beaten egg and draw up over the filling, pressing the edges well together to seal. Crimp between finger and thumb.

3 Transfer to a baking sheet. Brush with beaten egg to glaze and bake in the oven at 200°C/400°F/gas mark 6 for about 15–20 minutes until golden brown. Serve hot or cold with coleslaw and a green salad.

PREPARATION TIME: 10 MINUTES

COOKING TIME: 15–20 MINUTES

Midweek Beef Wellington

SERVES 4–6

	METRIC	IMPERIAL	AMERICAN
Large onion, chopped	1	1	1
Oil	15 ml	1 tbsp	1 tbsp
Can of sliced mushrooms, drained	300 g	11 oz	1 small
Sweet pickle	15 ml	1 tbsp	1 tbsp
Frozen puff pastry, thawed	450 g	1 lb	1 lb
Can of corned beef	350 g	12 oz	1 large
Egg, beaten	1	1	1

Sweetcorn (corn) and passata (sieved tomatoes), to serve

1 Fry (sauté) the onion in the oil for 3 minutes until softened but not browned. Stir in the mushrooms and sweet pickle and leave to cool.

2 Roll out the pastry to a rectangle about 25×18 cm/ 10×7 in.

3 Spoon the onion mixture into the centre of the pastry and place the corned beef on top.

4 Brush the edges of the pastry with beaten egg, fold over the filling and press well together to seal.

5 Place, sealed side, down on a dampened baking sheet.

6 Make a criss-cross pattern over the pastry with a sharp knife and brush all over with beaten egg.

7 Bake in the oven at 220°C/425°F/gas mark 7 for 30 minutes, covering lightly with foil if over-browning. Serve hot with sweetcorn and hot passata as a sauce.

PREPARATION TIME:
10 MINUTES

COOKING TIME:
33 MINUTES

Corned Beef-stuffed Pancakes

SERVES 4	METRIC	IMPERIAL	AMERICAN
Can of corned beef	350 g	12 oz	1 large
Tomato ketchup (catsup)	30 ml	2 tbsp	2 tbsp
Sweet pickle	15 ml	1 tbsp	1 tbsp
Packet of pancake batter mix	1	1	1
Egg, according to packet directions			
Milk or water, according to packet directions			
Oil for shallow-frying			
Packet of cheese sauce mix	1	1	1
Salad, to serve			

1 Chop the corned beef and mix it with the tomato ketchup and pickle. Heat gently until piping hot.

2 Meanwhile, make up the pancake batter with egg, if necessary, and 300 ml/½ pt/1¼ cups of liquid.

3 Heat a little oil in a frying pan (skillet) and pour off any excess. Add about 30 ml/2 tbsp of the batter and swirl round to coat the base of the pan. Fry (sauté) until the underside is golden. Turn over and brown the other side. Slide out of the pan and keep warm while cooking the remaining pancakes in same way.

4 Spread a little of the filling on each pancake, roll up and keep hot while making the sauce according to the packet directions with the remaining liquid. Pour over the pancakes and serve hot with salad.

PREPARATION TIME:
10 MINUTES

COOKING TIME:
ABOUT 30 MINUTES

Mediterranean Lamb Chops

If you want to go out, pop these in a moderate oven for an hour or longer instead of cooking them on top of the stove.

SERVES 4	METRIC	IMPERIAL	AMERICAN
Frozen lamb chops, thawed	4	4	4
Oil	15 ml	1 tbsp	1 tbsp
Onion, chopped	1	1	1
Salt and pepper			
Can of condensed tomato soup	295 g	10½ oz	1 small
Dried basil	5 ml	1 tsp	1 tsp
A few black olives, to garnish			
Buttered noodles, to serve			

1 Fry (sauté) the chops in the oil on each side to brown.

2 Remove from the pan and fry the onion for 3 minutes until soft and turning golden. Drain off the fat from the pan.

3 Return the chops to the pan with the onions, sprinkle with salt and pepper and spoon the soup over. Add the herbs.

4 Bring to the boil, reduce the heat, cover and simmer very gently for 45 minutes or until the chops are really tender. Stir gently occasionally and add a little water if necessary. Garnish with black olives and serve with buttered noodles.

PREPARATION TIME:
5 MINUTES

COOKING TIME:
45 MINUTES

Greek-style Lamb Lunch

SERVES 4	METRIC	IMPERIAL	AMERICAN
Frozen minced (ground) lamb steaks	4	4	4
Plain yoghurt	150 ml	¼ pt	⅔ cup
Garlic clove, crushed	1	1	1
Dried mint	5 ml	1 tsp	1 tsp
Salt and pepper			
Pitta breads	4	4	4
Shredded lettuce, grated cucumber and chopped tomato, to garnish			

1 Grill (broil), fry (sauté) or microwave the lamb steaks according to the packet instructions.

2 Meanwhile, mix the yoghurt with the garlic, mint and a little salt and pepper.

3 Grill or microwave the pittas to warm. Make a slit along one long edge of each and open up to form a pocket.

4 Put a lamb steak in each pocket. Spoon in the yoghurt mixture and garnish each with lettuce, cucumber and tomato.

PREPARATION TIME:
5 MINUTES

COOKING TIME:
ABOUT 10 MINUTES

Pan-casseroled Chicken

This dish is also excellent cooked in a moderate oven for about 1 hour.

SERVES 4	METRIC	IMPERIAL	AMERICAN
Frozen chicken portions, thawed	4	4	4
Plain (all-purpose) flour	30 ml	2 tbsp	2 tbsp
Salt and pepper			
Butter	40 g	1½ oz	3 tbsp
Curry powder or paste	5 ml	1 tsp	1 tsp
Can of condensed cream of mushroom soup	295 g	10½ oz	1 small
Plain boiled rice and Brussels sprouts, to serve			

1 Wipe the chicken with kitchen paper. Mix the flour with a little salt and pepper and use to coat the chicken.

2 Melt the butter in a flameproof casserole (Dutch oven) and fry (sauté) the chicken on all sides to brown.

3 Take the chicken out of the casserole. Drain off all but 15 ml/1 tbsp of the fat. Stir in the curry powder or paste and fry for 1 minute. Blend in the soup.

4 Return the chicken to the casserole, bring to the boil, reduce the heat to as low as possible, cover and simmer for 45 minutes until the chicken is tender. Stir occasionally and add a little water, if necessary, to prevent sticking. Serve with boiled rice and sprouts.

PREPARATION TIME:
5 MINUTES

COOKING TIME:
50 MINUTES

Chunky Chicken Parcels with Cranberry

SERVES 4	METRIC	IMPERIAL	AMERICAN
Filo pastry (paste) sheets	4	4	4
Butter, melted	50 g	2 oz	¼ cup
Can of chunky chicken	425 g	15 oz	1 large
Dried mixed herbs	5 ml	1 tsp	1 tsp
Cranberry sauce	60 ml	4 tbsp	4 tbsp
Port	15 ml	1 tbsp	1 tbsp

Parsley, to garnish

New potatoes and asparagus spears, to serve

1 Lay a pastry sheet on the work surface. Brush lightly with melted butter, fold in half, then brush again.

2 Put a quarter of the chicken in the centre of the pastry and sprinkle with 1.5 ml/¼ tsp herbs.

3 Draw the pastry up over the filling to form a pouch. Transfer to a buttered baking sheet and brush with melted butter. Repeat with the remaining ingredients.

4 Bake in the oven at 200°C/400°F/gas mark 6 for 10–15 minutes until golden brown.

5 Meanwhile, heat the cranberry sauce and port together in a saucepan. Transfer the chicken parcels to warm serving plates. Spoon a little of the sauce around each and garnish with parsley before serving with new potatoes and asparagus spears.

PREPARATION TIME:
8 MINUTES

COOKING TIME:
10–15 MINUTES

Rosy Chicken Salad

SERVES 4–6	METRIC	IMPERIAL	AMERICAN
Whole ready-cooked chicken	1.5 kg	3 lb	3 lb
Mayonnaise	150 ml	¼ pt	⅔ cup
Milk	15 ml	1 tbsp	1 tbsp
Tomato purée (paste)	15 ml	1 tbsp	1 tbsp
Piece of cucumber, finely diced	5 cm	2 in	2 in
Blanched whole almonds	50 g	2 oz	½ cup
Butter or margarine	15 g	½ oz	1 tbsp
Chilli powder	1.5 ml	¼ tsp	¼ tsp
Mixed (apple-pie) spice	1.5 ml	¼ tsp	¼ tsp
Lettuce, to garnish			
Potatoes boiled in their skins and salad, to serve			

1 Joint the chicken into six pieces and carve the breast.
   Alternatively, cut all the meat off the bones, discard
   the skin and leave the meat in chunky pieces.

2 Blend together the mayonnaise, milk, tomato purée
   and cucumber.

3 Fry (sauté) the almonds in the butter until golden
   brown. Sprinkle with the spices and toss well. Drain
   on kitchen paper.

4 Arrange the chicken attractively on a bed of lettuce.
   Spoon the mayonnaise mixture over and scatter with
   the almonds. Serve with potatoes and salad.

PREPARATION TIME:
10 MINUTES

COOKING TIME:
ABOUT 3 MINUTES
(FOR ALMONDS)

Mock Peking Duck

You will find Chinese pancakes in the chill cabinet near the poultry and flour tortillas near the pitta breads and bagels. Alternatively, use pittas and fill rather than roll up.

SERVES 4	METRIC	IMPERIAL	AMERICAN
Bunch of spring onions (scallions)	1	1	1
Cucumber	¼	¼	¼
Turkey stir-fry pieces	450 g	1 lb	1 lb
Chinese pancakes or flour tortillas	12	12	12
Oil	15 ml	1 tbsp	1 tbsp
Marinade:			
Soy sauce	30 ml	2 tbsp	2 tbsp
Ground ginger	2.5 ml	½ tsp	½ tsp
Garlic clove, crushed	1	1	1
Red wine vinegar	15 ml	1 tbsp	1 tbsp
Pepper			
Plum sauce:			
Plum jam (conserve)	60 ml	4 tbsp	4 tbsp
Soy sauce	30 ml	2 tbsp	2 tbsp
Ground ginger	5 ml	1 tsp	1 tsp
Lemon juice	5 ml	1 tsp	1 tsp

1 Trim the roots and tops off the spring onions and make several cuts from the root ends to the stems. Place in a bowl of cold water in the fridge.

2 Cut the cucumber into thin strips. Place in a serving bowl and chill.

3 Put the turkey in a shallow dish. Mix together the marinade ingredients and pour over. Leave to stand for at least 1 hour.

4 Mix the plum jam with the soy sauce, ginger and lemon juice. Put in a small serving bowl. Warm the pancakes or tortillas either on a covered plate over a pan of boiling water or in the microwave.

5 Heat the oil in a large frying pan (skillet) or a wok. Drain the turkey and stir-fry for about 5 minutes until cooked through. Turn into a serving dish.

6 Drain the onions and pat dry.

7 To serve, use a spring onion 'brush' to dip in the plum sauce and spread sauce over a pancake or tortilla. Add a spoonful of meat and some cucumber. Roll up and eat with your fingers.

PREPARATION TIME:
10 MINUTES
PLUS MARINATING TIME

COOKING TIME:
5 MINUTES

Maybe Chicken Chow Mein

SERVES 4	METRIC	IMPERIAL	AMERICAN
Quick-cook Chinese egg noodles	225 g	8 oz	8 oz
Cooked chicken, cut into strips	225 g	8 oz	2 cups
Can of stir-fry mixed vegetables, drained	425 g	15 oz	1 large
Garlic clove, crushed	1	1	1
Soy sauce	30 ml	2 tbsp	2 tbsp
Sherry	30 ml	2 tbsp	2 tbsp
Ground ginger	5 ml	1 tsp	1 tsp
Brown sugar	15 ml	1 tbsp	1 tbsp
Cashew nuts (optional), to garnish			

1 Cook the noodles according to the packet directions. Drain.

2 Put all the remaining ingredients in a large pan or wok and heat through, stirring occasionally, until piping hot.

3 Stir in the noodles, reheat and serve garnished with cashew nuts, if liked.

PREPARATION TIME: 10 MINUTES COOKING TIME: 10 MINUTES

Oriental Chicken Loaf

SERVES 4–6	METRIC	IMPERIAL	AMERICAN
Cooked chicken, minced (ground)	350 g	12 oz	3 cups
Minced onion	75 g	3 oz	¾ cup
Can of crushed pineapple	440 g	15½ oz	1 large
Canned pimiento cap, chopped	1	1	1
Soy sauce	15 ml	1 tbsp	1 tbsp
Packets of bread sauce mix	2	2	2
Salt and pepper			
Eggs, beaten	2	2	2

Canned bean sprouts with grated cucumber and carrot
  in an oil, vinegar and soy sauce dressing, to serve

1 Mix together the chicken, onion, pineapple, pimiento, soy sauce, bread sauce mix and salt and pepper to taste. Bind together with the eggs and place in a lightly greased loaf tin (pan).

2 Cover with a double thickness of foil and steam for 1 hour. Leave to cool.

3 Turn out on to a serving dish and serve cold, cut into slices, with a bean sprout, carrot and cucumber salad.

PREPARATION TIME:
5 MINUTES

COOKING TIME:
1 HOUR
PLUS COOLING TIME

Cheat Chicken Maryland

SERVES 4	METRIC	IMPERIAL	AMERICAN
Frozen crumb-coated chicken nuggets	450 g	1 lb	1 lb
Streaky bacon rashers (slices)	4–8	4–8	4–8
Large bananas	2	2	2
Oil for shallow-frying			
Corn fritters (page 26)			
New potatoes and green salad, to serve			

1 Grill (broil) or fry (sauté) the chicken nuggets according to the packet directions. Keep warm.

2 Cut the bacon rashers in half, roll up and grill or fry until cooked through. Keep warm.

3 Halve each banana lengthways, then across to make eight pieces in all. Fry in a little oil until just softening. Serve with the chicken, bacon, corn fritters, new potatoes and a green salad.

PREPARATION TIME:
5 MINUTES
PLUS MAKING
CORN FRITTERS

COOKING TIME:
20 MINUTES

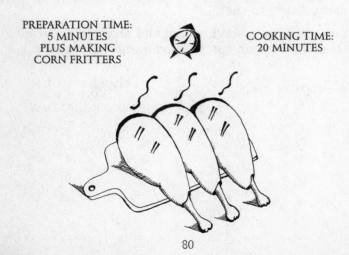

Chicken and Vegetable Mornay

Substitute tuna for the chicken, if preferred.

SERVES 4	METRIC	IMPERIAL	AMERICAN
Packet of cheese sauce mix	1	1	1
Milk or water, according to packet directions			
Cooked leftover vegetables, chopped (or frozen vegetables, cooked)	350 g	12 oz	3 cups
Cooked chicken, diced	175 g	6 oz	1½ cups
Grated nutmeg	1.5 ml	¼ tsp	¼ tsp
Cheddar cheese, grated	50 g	2 oz	½ cup
Garlic bread (see Garlic Butter, page 157), to serve			

1 Make up the cheese sauce according to the packet directions.

2 Stir in the vegetables, chicken and nutmeg. Heat through for 3 minutes, stirring occasionally.

3 Turn into a 1.2 litre/2 oz/5 cup flameproof dish. Sprinkle with the grated cheese and grill (broil) for 5 minutes until the cheese is melted and turning golden. Serve hot with garlic bread.

PREPARATION TIME:
3 MINUTES

COOKING TIME:
ABOUT 10 MINUTES

Quick Cassoulet

SERVES 4–6	METRIC	IMPERIAL	AMERICAN
Bacon rashers (slices) or cooked ham slices, diced	4	4	4
Can of hot dog sausages, drained and cut into chunks	400 g	14 oz	1 large
Can of red kidney beans, drained	425 g	15 oz	1 large
Can of baked beans in tomato sauce	425 g	15 oz	1 large
Can of cut green beans, drained	275 g	10 oz	1 small
Crusty bread, to serve			

1 If using bacon, dry-fry (sauté) in a large saucepan.

2 Stir in the remaining ingredients. Heat through for about 5 minutes, stirring gently from time to time, until piping hot. Serve in soup bowls with crusty bread.

PREPARATION TIME: 2 MINUTES

COOKING TIME: ABOUT 7 MINUTES

Barbecued Bangers

SERVES 4	METRIC	IMPERIAL	AMERICAN
Chipolata sausages	450 g	1 lb	1 lb
Butter or margarine	15 g	½ oz	1 tbsp
Lemon juice	15 ml	1 tbsp	1 tbsp
Red wine vinegar	15 ml	1 tbsp	1 tbsp
Tomato purée (paste)	30 ml	2 tbsp	2 tbsp
Brown table sauce	15 ml	1 tbsp	1 tbsp
Golden (light corn) syrup	30 ml	2 tbsp	2 tbsp
Boiled rice and peas, to serve			

1 Dry-fry (sauté) the sausages in a large frying pan (skillet) for about 10 minutes until cooked through and browned all over.

2 Heat together the remaining ingredients in a saucepan. Pour over the sausages and cook for a further 3 minutes until the sausages are coated in a sticky sauce.

3 Serve with boiled rice and peas.

PREPARATION TIME:
2 MINUTES

COOKING TIME:
13 MINUTES

Smoked Cheese and Frankfurter Flan

SERVES 4–6	METRIC	IMPERIAL	AMERICAN
Shortcrust pastry (basic pie crust)	225 g	8 oz	8 oz
Onion, chopped	1	1	1
Oil	15 ml	1 tbsp	1 tbsp
Can of chopped tomatoes	225 g	8 oz	1 small
Ground cinnamon	2.5 ml	½ tsp	½ tsp
Tomato purée (paste)	15 ml	1 tbsp	1 tbsp
Frankfurters, canned or vacuum-packed	5	5	5
Smoked cheese roll	100 g	4 oz	4 oz
Salad and jacket potatoes, to serve			

1 Roll out the pastry and use to line a 23 cm/9 in flan dish (pie pan). Prick the base with a fork, line with crumpled foil and bake 'blind' in the oven at 190°C/375°F/gas mark 5 for 10 minutes. Remove the foil and return to the oven for 5 minutes to dry out.

2 Meanwhile, fry (sauté) the onion in the oil for 3 minutes until soft but not browned. Add the tomatoes, cinnamon and tomato purée and simmer for 10 minutes. Chop the frankfurters, add to the sauce and turn into the flan case (pie shell).

3 Slice the cheese and arrange in a ring around the top.

4 Bake in the oven at the same temperature for 15 minutes until the cheese is golden and the flan is hot through. Serve hot or cold with salad and jacket potatoes.

PREPARATION TIME:
5 MINUTES

COOKING TIME:
38 MINUTES

Sauerkraut with Frankfurters

SERVES 4	METRIC	IMPERIAL	AMERICAN
Jar of sauerkraut	670 g	1 lb 6 oz	1 large
Caraway seeds	15 ml	1 tbsp	1 tbsp
Frankfurters, vacuum-packed or canned	12	12	12

Plain boiled potatoes and German or Dijon mustard, to serve

1 Empty the sauerkraut into a saucepan. Add the caraway seeds and heat through. Drain.

2 Heat the frankfurters according to the packet directions.

3 Serve on warm plates with plain boiled potatoes and mustard.

PREPARATION TIME:
4 MINUTES

COOKING TIME:
8 MINUTES

Ham in Puff Pastry

SERVES 6	METRIC	IMPERIAL	AMERICAN
Frozen puff pastry (paste), thawed	450 g	1 lb	1 lb
Cans of ham	2×450 g	2×1 lb	2 large
Can of creamed mushrooms	215 g	7½ oz	1 small
Dried marjoram or oregano	10 ml	2 tsp	2 tsp
Egg, beaten	1	1	1
Redcurrant jelly (clear conserve)	45 ml	3 tbsp	3 tbsp
Orange juice	45 ml	3 tbsp	3 tbsp
Parsley, to garnish			
New potatoes and green beans, to serve			

1 Cut the pastry into six equal pieces and roll out each to a square about 18–20 cm/7–8 in. Trim the edges.

2 Cut each can of ham into three slices, discarding the jelly.

3 Divide the mushrooms between the centres of the pastry. Sprinkle with the herbs, then top each with a slice of ham.

4 Brush the edges of the pastry with beaten egg. Fold over the filling to form parcels.

5 Place, folds down, on a dampened baking sheet. Make 'leaves' out of the pastry trimmings and arrange on the parcels. Brush with beaten egg to glaze.

6 Bake in the oven at 220°C/425°F/gas mark 7 for 12–15 minutes until golden brown.

7 Meanwhile, heat the redcurrant jelly with the orange juice in a saucepan until it has dissolved.

8 Transfer the ham parcels to warm serving plates, spoon a little sauce to the side of each and garnish with parsley. Serve hot with potatoes and green beans.

PREPARATION TIME:
15 MINUTES

COOKING TIME:
12–15 MINUTES

Grilled Ham with Pineapple

SERVES 4

Can of ham	450 g	1 lb	1 large
Can of chopped tomatoes, drained	225 g	8 oz	1 small
Cheddar cheese, grated	75 g	3 oz	¾ cup
Canned pineapple slices	4	4	4
French fries and peas, to serve			

1 Cut ham into four steaks, discarding the jelly. Place on a grill (broiler) pan and grill (broil) for 1 minute on each side.

2 Spoon the tomatoes over, top with grated cheese and place a pineapple slice on each.

3 Return to the grill and cook until hot through and the cheese is bubbling and the top is turning golden. Serve hot with French fries and peas.

PREPARATION TIME:
2 MINUTES

COOKING TIME:
7 MINUTES

Sausage Salad

SERVES 4–6	METRIC	IMPERIAL	AMERICAN
Slices of white bread, cubed	4	4	4
Oil	45 ml	3 tbsp	3 tbsp
Thick sausages, cooked and sliced	8	8	8
Cans of sweetcorn (corn) with (bell) peppers, drained	2×320 g	2×12 oz	2 large
Can of butter beans, drained	425 g	15 oz	1 large
Cucumber, diced	½	½	½
Bunch of radishes, trimmed and quartered (optional)	1	1	1
Garlic clove, crushed	1	1	1
Plain yoghurt or soured (dairy sour) cream	150 ml	¼ pt	⅔ cup
Dried chives	15 ml	1 tbsp	1 tbsp

1 Fry (sauté) the cubes of bread in the hot oil until golden. Drain on kitchen paper.

2 Mix the sausages with the corn, butter beans, cucumber and radishes, if using. Chill until ready to serve.

3 Mix the garlic with the yoghurt or soured cream and chives. Chill.

4 Just before serving, add the fried bread to the salad and toss. Pile on to serving plates and top with a spoonful of the creamy dressing. Serve immediately.

PREPARATION TIME:
10 MINUTES
PLUS CHILLING

VEGETARIAN MEALS

You don't have to be a whole-hearted
vegetarian to enjoy meatless meals. All the
following are tasty, nutritious dishes for all
the family – and so simple. Never be afraid
to experiment with your own ideas as well, or
quick and easy suggestions such as slicing
some dill pickles on to granary bread,
topping with your favourite cheese and
grilling until hot and bubbling.

Stuffed Pizzas

SERVES 4	METRIC	IMPERIAL	AMERICAN
Pizza base mixes	2	2	2
Can of creamed mushrooms	215 g	7½ oz	1 small
Can of chopped tomatoes, drained	225 g	8 oz	1 small
Canned pimiento cap, chopped (optional)	1	1	1
Capers	5 ml	1 tsp	1 tsp
Cooked peas or green beans	15 ml	1 tbsp	1 tbsp
Grated Mozzarella or Cheddar cheese	60 ml	4 tbsp	4 tbsp
Passata (sieved tomatoes) and extra grated Parmesan cheese, to garnish			

1 Make up the pizza mixes according to the packet directions.

2 Knead the dough gently and cut into quarters. Roll out each piece, or flatten between the hands, to a round about 20 cm/8 in in diameter.

3 Divide all the filling ingredients between the centres of the rounds of dough. Brush the edges with water and draw up over the filling to seal.

4 Place sealed-sides down on a lightly greased baking sheet. Bake in the oven at 200°C/400°F/gas mark 6 for about 20 minutes or until golden brown.

5 Transfer to warm serving plates. Spoon a little hot passata over, sprinkle with Parmesan cheese and serve.

PREPARATION TIME:
10 MINUTES

COOKING TIME:
ABOUT 20 MINUTES

Pasta Surprise

SERVES 4	METRIC	IMPERIAL	AMERICAN
Pasta shapes	225 g	8 oz	8 oz
Passata (sieved tomatoes)	300 ml	½ pt	1¼ cups
Can of sweetcorn (corn)	200 g	7 oz	1 small
Dried oregano	2.5 ml	½ tsp	½ tsp
Salt and pepper			
Frozen chopped spinach	225 g	8 oz	8 oz
Packet of cheese sauce mix	1	1	1
Milk or water, according to packet directions			
Cheddar or Parmesan cheese, grated (optional)	50 g	2 oz	½ cup

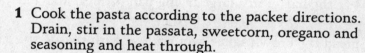

1 Cook the pasta according to the packet directions. Drain, stir in the passata, sweetcorn, oregano and seasoning and heat through.

2 Cook the spinach according to the packet directions. Drain if necessary.

3 Make up the cheese sauce according to the packet directions.

4 Put half the pasta mixture into the base of a 1.2 litre/2 pt/5 cup flameproof dish. Top with the spinach, then the remaining pasta.

5 Spoon the sauce over, cover with grated cheese, if using, and brown under a hot grill (broiler) for about 5 minutes. Serve hot.

PREPARATION TIME:
5 MINUTES

COOKING TIME:
15 MINUTES

Egg and Vegetable Platter

SERVES 4	METRIC	IMPERIAL	AMERICAN
Cooked leftover vegetables, including potatoes (or cooked frozen vegetables and a little prepared instant mash)	*350 g*	*12 oz*	*12 oz*
Pepper			
Butter	*15 g*	*½ oz*	*1 tbsp*
Brown table sauce	*15 ml*	*1 tbsp*	*1 tbsp*
Eggs	*4*	*4*	*4*
A little oil			

1 Chop the vegetables and season lightly with pepper. Melt the butter in a large frying pan (skillet) and add half the vegetables. Press down flat.

2 Spread the brown sauce over the top with the remaining vegetables, again pressing down well.

3 Cover with a plate and cook gently for about 15 minutes. Loosen the base and turn out on to a plate. Cut into quarters.

4 Meanwhile, fry (sauté) the eggs in the oil (or poach in water). Slide one egg on top of each quarter and serve hot.

PREPARATION TIME: 3 MINUTES

COOKING TIME: 15 MINUTES

Spinach and Mushroom Roll

SERVES 4	METRIC	IMPERIAL	AMERICAN
Frozen spinach, thawed	300 g	11 oz	11 oz
Pinch of grated nutmeg			
Eggs, separated	4	4	4
Salt and pepper			
Can of creamed mushrooms	215 g	7½ oz	1 small
Hot passata (sieved tomatoes) or Quick Tomato Sauce (page 152) and buttered noodles, to serve			

1 Grease and line an 18×28 cm/7×11 in Swiss roll tin (jelly roll pan) and line with baking parchment.

2 Cook the spinach according to the packet directions. Drain well. Add the nutmeg and egg yolks and beat well. Season with a little salt and pepper.

3 Whisk the egg whites until stiff. Fold into the spinach mixture with a metal spoon. Turn into the prepared tin.

4 Bake in the oven at 200°C/400°F/gas mark 6 for 20 minutes or until just firm to the touch.

5 Heat the creamed mushrooms.

6 Turn the spinach mixture out on to a clean sheet of baking parchment. Quickly spread with the creamed mushrooms and roll up, using the parchment to help.

7 Transfer to a serving plate and serve with hot passata or tomato sauce and buttered noodles.

PREPARATION TIME:
10 MINUTES

COOKING TIME:
25 MINUTES

The Fastest Soufflé in the West

SERVES 4	METRIC	IMPERIAL	AMERICAN
Butter, for greasing			
Can of sliced mushrooms, drained	300 g	11 oz	1 small
Can of condensed cream of mushroom soup	295 g	10½ oz	1 small
Cheddar or Parmesan cheese, grated	75 g	3 oz	¾ cup
Eggs, separated	4	4	4
Black pepper			
Salad, to serve			

1 Grease an 18 cm/7 in soufflé dish with the butter.

2 Put the mushrooms in the base of the dish.

3 Empty the soup into a bowl. Whisk in the cheese and egg yolks. Season with pepper.

4 Whisk the egg whites until stiff. Fold into the soup mixture with a metal spoon.

5 Turn into the dish and bake in the oven at 200°C/400°F/gas mark 6 for 25–30 minutes until risen, golden and just set. Serve immediately with a salad.

PREPARATION TIME: 4 MINUTES COOKING TIME: 25–30 MINUTES

Variations

Use any combination you like: Try:

- Drained asparagus tips with asparagus soup
- Baked beans, ratatouille or cut celery with celery soup

Savoury Eggy Rice

SERVES 2–4	METRIC	IMPERIAL	AMERICAN
Packet of savoury rice	1	1	1
Eggs	4	4	4
Garlic bread (see Garlic Butter, page 157), to serve			

1 Empty the packet of rice into a large frying pan (skillet). Add water as directed and bring to the boil. Cover with a lid and simmer for 15 minutes.

2 Remove the lid and stir. Make four 'wells' in the rice mixture, break an egg into each, cover and continue cooking over a gentle heat for 5 minutes or until the eggs are set. Serve straight from the pan with garlic bread.

PREPARATION TIME:
2 MINUTES

COOKING TIME:
20 MINUTES

Bean Stew with Dumplings

SERVES 4–6	METRIC	IMPERIAL	AMERICAN
Can of butter beans, drained	425 g	15 oz	1 large
Can of black-eyed beans, drained	425 g	15 oz	1 large
Can of chopped tomatoes	400 g	14 oz	1 large
Garlic clove, crushed	1	1	1
Tomato purée (paste)	15 ml	1 tbsp	1 tbsp
Can of sweetcorn (corn) with (bell) peppers	200 g	7 oz	1 small
Can of cut green beans	275 g	10 oz	1 small
Vegetable stock	300 ml	½ pt	1¼ cups
Bay leaf	1	1	1
Salt and pepper			
Packet of dumpling mix	1	1	1
Cheddar cheese, grated	50 g	2 oz	½ cup
Dried mixed herbs	2.5 ml	½ tsp	½ tsp

1 Empty the drained butter and black-eyed beans into a saucepan with the tomatoes, garlic, tomato purée, the contents of the cans of sweetcorn and green beans (not drained), the stock, bay leaf and a little salt and pepper. Bring to the boil, reduce the heat, cover and simmer for 5 minutes. Discard the bay leaf.

2 Meanwhile, empty the dumpling mix into a bowl with the cheese and herbs. Add enough cold water to form a soft but not sticky dough. Shape into eight balls.

3 Arrange the dumplings around the top of the stew, cover and simmer for about 15–20 minutes until fluffy. Serve hot.

PREPARATION TIME:
4 MINUTES

COOKING TIME:
20–25 MINUTES

Broccoli and Cider Cheese

SERVES 4	METRIC	IMPERIAL	AMERICAN
Frozen broccoli	350 g	12 oz	12 oz
Packet of cheese sauce mix	1	1	1
Cider	300 ml	½ pt	1¼ cups
Cheddar cheese, grated	50 g	2 oz	½ cup
Grilled (broiled) tomatoes and crusty bread, to serve			

1 Cook the broccoli according to the packet directions. Drain and arrange in a fairly shallow flameproof dish.

2 Make up the cheese sauce using cider instead of milk or water. Pour over the broccoli and top with the grated cheese.

3 Place under a hot grill (broiler) for about 5 minutes until golden brown and bubbling. Serve with grilled tomatoes and crusty bread.

PREPARATION TIME:
2 MINUTES

COOKING TIME:
10 MINUTES

Omelette in the Fingers

SERVES 2–4	METRIC	IMPERIAL	AMERICAN
Eggs	4	4	4
Cold water	60 ml	4 tbsp	4 tbsp
Salt and pepper			
Dried mixed herbs	5 ml	1 tsp	1 tsp
Butter for shallow-frying			
Can of asparagus spears, drained	295 g	10½ oz	1 small
Crusty bread and chunky salad pieces, to serve			

1 Beat one egg in a bowl with 15 ml/1 tbsp water, a little salt and pepper and 1.5 ml/¼ tsp of the herbs.

2 Heat a little butter in an omelette pan. Pour in the egg and fry (sauté), lifting the edge and letting uncooked egg run underneath until set. Transfer to a plate and leave to cool while making three more omelettes in the same way.

3 Divide the asparagus spears between the omelettes. Roll up and serve with crusty bread and chunky salad pieces that can be eaten in the fingers.

PREPARATION TIME:
2 MINUTES

COOKING TIME:
ABOUT 10 MINUTES
PLUS COOLING TIME

Waldorf Grill

SERVES 4	METRIC	IMPERIAL	AMERICAN
Can of celery hearts, drained	515 g	18½ oz	1 large
Eating (dessert) apple, thinly sliced	1	1	1
Packet of cheese sauce mix	1	1	1
Milk or water, according to packet directions			
Walnut pieces, chopped	50 g	2 oz	½ cup
Cheddar cheese, grated	50 g	2 oz	½ cup
Jacket potatoes, to serve			

1 Empty the celery into a flameproof casserole (Dutch oven). Add the apple slices. Bring to the boil, simmer for 2 minutes, then drain off the liquid.

2 Meanwhile, make up the cheese sauce according to the packet directions. Stir in the walnuts.

3 Pour the sauce over the celery and apple. Cover with the grated cheese. Place under a hot grill (broiler) for about 5 minutes until golden and bubbling. Serve hot with jacket potatoes.

PREPARATION TIME:
3 MINUTES

COOKING TIME:
ABOUT 10 MINUTES

Fluffy Cheese Pudding

SERVES 4	METRIC	IMPERIAL	AMERICAN
Butter	25 g	1 oz	2 tbsp
Eggs, separated	2	2	2
Milk	300 ml	½ pt	1¼ cups
Fresh breadcrumbs	75 g	3 oz	1½ cups
Cheddar cheese, grated	100 g	4 oz	1 cup
Salt and pepper			
Baked fresh or canned tomatoes, to serve			

1 Grease a 1.2 litre/2 pt/5 cup ovenproof dish well with the butter.

2 Beat the egg yolks with the milk and stir in the breadcrumbs, cheese and a little salt and pepper. Leave to stand for 15 minutes.

3 Whisk the egg whites until stiff and fold into the mixture with a metal spoon. Turn into the prepared dish.

4 Cook in the oven at 200°C/400°F/gas mark 6 for 35 minutes until risen and golden. Serve immediately with baked fresh or canned tomatoes.

PREPARATION TIME:
3 MINUTES
PLUS STANDING TIME

COOKING TIME:
35 MINUTES

Mixed Vegetable Fritters with Garlic Mayonnaise

SERVES 4	METRIC	IMPERIAL	AMERICAN
Garlic cloves, crushed	3	3	3
Mayonnaise	150 ml	¼ pt	⅔ cup
Black pepper and salt			
Plain (all-purpose) flour	75 g	3 oz	¾ cup
Tepid water	120 ml	4 fl oz	½ cup
Oil	15 ml	1 tbsp	1 tbsp
Can of mixed vegetables, thoroughly drained	275 g	10 oz	1 small
Egg white	1	1	1
Oil for deep-frying			

1 Mix the garlic with the mayonnaise and a little seasoning. Cover well and chill until ready to serve.

2 To make the fritters, mix the flour with the water and measured oil until smooth. Stir in the vegetables.

3 Whisk the egg white until stiff and fold into the batter with a metal spoon.

4 Heat the oil until a cube of day-old bread browns in 30 seconds. Deep-fry spoonfuls of the mixture, a few at a time, until crisp and golden. Drain on kitchen paper and serve hot with the chilled garlic sauce.

PREPARATION TIME: 5 MINUTES

COOKING TIME: ABOUT 20 MINUTES

Stuffed Cabbage Leaves

SERVES 4	METRIC	IMPERIAL	AMERICAN
Large cabbage leaves	8	8	8
Can ratatouille	425 g	15 oz	1 large
Cooked long-grain rice	60 ml	4 tbsp	4 tbsp
Vegetable stock	300 ml	½ pt	1¼ cups
Passata (sieved tomatoes)	45 ml	3 tbsp	3 tbsp
Salt and pepper			
Grated Cheddar cheese and crusty bread, to serve			

1 Cut out the thick central base stalk from each leaf.

2 Put the leaves in a pan of boiling water and cook for 3–4 minutes to soften. Drain, rinse with cold water and drain again.

3 Mix the ratatouille with the rice.

4 Dry the leaves with kitchen paper. Lay upside-down on a board and overlap the two points where the stalk was. Put a good spoonful of filling on top. Fold in the sides, then roll up.

5 Pack into the base of a lightly greased heavy flameproof casserole (Dutch oven).

6 Mix the stock with the passata and pour over. Sprinkle with a little salt and pepper. Bring to the boil, reduce the heat, cover and simmer for about 20 minutes or until the cabbage is tender.

7 Serve hot with grated cheese and crusty bread.

PREPARATION TIME: 3 MINUTES

COOKING TIME: 24 MINUTES

DESSERTS

No meal is complete unless it is rounded off
with something sweet, exciting and utterly
delicious. Well, now you can do tons better
than the chill cabinet at the supermarket –
there's a whole range of fantastic desserts
just waiting to burst out of your store
cupboard! Some of the best ideas are the
simplest. To create a Chocolate Orange
Sundae in minutes, stir 60 ml/4 tbsp of
chocolate spread into 300 ml/½ pt/1¼ cups of
whipped cream, then layer it into wine goblets
with a can of drained mandarin oranges.
Chill and serve sprinkled with a few toasted
nuts. Now for a whole host more ideas …

Peach Fool

SERVES 4	METRIC	IMPERIAL	AMERICAN
Can of peach slices, drained with the juice reserved	410 g	14½ oz	1 large
Can of custard	425 g	15 oz	1 large
Plain yoghurt	150 ml	¼ pt	⅔ cup
Glacé (candied) cherries, to decorate			

1 Blend or purée the peaches in a food processor.

2 Fold in the custard until well blended.

3 Fold in the yoghurt until there is a marbled effect.

4 Spoon into glasses. Chill. Top each with a glacé cherry and a little of the reserved juice just before serving.

PREPARATION TIME:
3 MINUTES
PLUS CHILLING TIME

The Best Custard Tart

SERVES 4–6	METRIC	IMPERIAL	AMERICAN
Shortcrust pastry (basic pie crust)	175 g	6 oz	6 oz
Eggs	2	2	2
Milk	150 ml	¼ pt	⅔ cup
Can of custard	425 g	15 oz	1 large
Caster (superfine) sugar	25 g	1 oz	2 tbsp
A little grated nutmeg			

⊠

1 Roll out the pastry and use to line a 20 cm/8 in flan dish (pie pan), set on a baking sheet.

2 Beat the eggs with the milk, then stir in all the remaining ingredients except the nutmeg. Pour into the flan case (pie shell).

3 Sprinkle a little nutmeg over, then bake in the oven at 190°C/375°F/gas mark 5 for about 40 minutes or until set. Serve warm or cold.

PREPARATION TIME:
5 MINUTES

COOKING TIME:
40 MINUTES

Honey Nut Bomb

SERVES 6	METRIC	IMPERIAL	AMERICAN
Soft-scoop vanilla ice cream	1 litre	1¾ pts	4¼ cups
Grated rind and juice of 1 lemon			
Clear honey	45 ml	3 tbsp	3 tbsp
Chopped toasted nuts	50 g	2 oz	½ cup
Crystallised (candied) lemon slices, to decorate			

1 Put the ice cream in a bowl. Quickly fold in the lemon rind and juice, the honey and nuts to give a marbled effect. Don't overmix or the ice cream will melt.

2 Pack in a 1 litre/1¾ pt/4¼ cup pudding basin. Cover and freeze until firm.

3 Loosen round the edge with a knife warmed in hot water, turn out and serve straight away decorated with crystallised lemon slices.

PREPARATION TIME:
5 MINUTES
PLUS FREEZING TIME

Variations:
Make an Italian Cassata in the same way by stirring a small jar of chopped Maraschino cherries and 50 g/2 oz of grated plain (semi-sweet) chocolate into the ice-cream. A Chocolate Ripple Ring is easily created by rippling a few tablespoons of chocolate hazelnut spread softened with some coffee liqueur into the ice-cream and pressing into a ring mould before freezing.

Caribbean Cooler

SERVES 6	METRIC	IMPERIAL	AMERICAN
Soft-scoop chocolate ice cream	1 litre	1¾ pts	4¼ cups
Bananas, mashed with lemon juice	2	2	2
Crystallised (candied) or stem ginger, very finely chopped	25 g	1 oz	2 tbsp
Grated chocolate, to decorate			

❁

1 Put the ice cream in a bowl. Quickly work in the bananas and ginger until just mixed. Don't overmix or the ice cream will start to melt.

2 Pack into a 450 g/1 lb loaf tin (pan). Wrap and freeze until firm.

3 To serve, stand the base of the tin briefly in hot water. Loosen round the edges with a knife and turn out. Decorate with grated chocolate and serve cut in slices.

PREPARATION TIME:
5 MINUTES
PLUS FREEZING TIME

Rum and Raisin Mountain

SERVES 6	METRIC	IMPERIAL	AMERICAN
Raisins	50 g	2 oz	⅓ cup
Rum	30 ml	2 tbsp	2 tbsp
Meringues, crushed	2–3	2–3	2–3
Soft-scoop vanilla ice cream	1 litre	1¾ pts	4¼ cups
Whipped cream, to decorate			

1 Put the raisins in a bowl. Add the rum and leave to soak for at least 1 hour.

2 Mash the soaked raisins into the ice cream, then stir in the crushed meringues. Work quickly to prevent the ice cream from melting.

3 Pack into a 1 litre/1¾ pt/4¼ cup pudding basin. Cover and freeze until firm.

4 Loosen round the edge with a warmed knife. Turn out on to a serving plate and pile whipped cream on top. Serve immediately.

PREPARATION TIME:
5 MINUTES
PLUS SOAKING AND
FREEZING TIME

Mock Rum Babas

SERVES 6	METRIC	IMPERIAL	AMERICAN
Granulated sugar	100 g	4 oz	½ cup
Water	150 ml	¼ pt	⅔ cup
Rum or rum essence (extract) and water	30 ml	2 tbsp	2 tbsp
Ring doughnuts	6	6	6
Whipped cream and chopped nuts, to decorate			

1 Dissolve the sugar in the water. Boil for 5 minutes until syrupy.

2 Stir in the rum or a few drops of rum essence made up to 30 ml/2 tbsp with water.

3 Prick the doughnuts all over with a skewer and spoon the rum syrup over them. Leave to soak in well.

4 Fill the centres with whipped cream, decorate with nuts and chill, if time allows, before serving.

PREPARATION TIME: 2 MINUTES

COOKING TIME: 5 MINUTES PLUS CHILLING TIME

Fruit Parcels

MAKES ABOUT 8	METRIC	IMPERIAL	AMERICAN
Filo pastry (paste) sheets (approx) 8	8	8	8
Butter, melted	75 g	3 oz	⅓ cup
Can of peach or pear halves	410 g	14½ oz	1 large
Jar of mincemeat	450 g	1 lb	1 small

1 For each parcel, brush a sheet of filo pastry with a little butter. Fold in half and brush again.

2 Drain the fruit, reserving the juice. Place a peach or pear half in the centre of each pastry sheet and top with a spoonful of mincemeat.

3 Draw the pastry up over the filling to form a parcel. Transfer to a buttered baking sheet and brush the pastry with a little more melted butter. Repeat with the remaining ingredients.

4 Bake in the oven at 200°C/400°F/gas mark 6 for about 15 minutes until golden brown.

5 Serve hot or cold with a little of the reserved juice.

PREPARATION TIME: 10 MINUTES

COOKING TIME: 15 MINUTES

Lemon Velvet

SERVES 4

	METRIC	IMPERIAL	AMERICAN
Packet of lemon meringue pie filling mix	1	1	1
Water	300 ml	½ pt	1¼ cups
Grated rind and juice of 1 lemon (or a little bottled lemon juice)			
Cold milk	150 ml	¼ pt	⅔ cup
Packet of Dream Topping mix	1	1	1
Crystallised (candied) lemon slices, to decorate	4	4	4

1 Blend the lemon meringue pie mix with the water in a saucepan. Bring to the boil, stirring until thickened. Stir in the lemon rind and juice and leave to cool.

2 Put the milk in a bowl. Add the Dream Topping and whisk until thick and fluffy.

3 Fold into the cold lemon mixture. Pile into four glasses and decorate each with a crystallised lemon slice before serving.

PREPARATION TIME:
6 MINUTES

COOKING TIME:
3 MINUTES
PLUS COOLING TIME

Chocolate Cups

SERVES 6	METRIC	IMPERIAL	AMERICAN
Whipping cream	*150 ml*	*¼ pt*	*⅔ cup*
Chocolate hazelnut spread	*30 ml*	*2 tbsp*	*2 tbsp*
Brandy, sherry, rum or whisky	*15 ml*	*1 tbsp*	*1 tbsp*
Ready-made chocolate shells	*6*	*6*	*6*

Toasted chopped hazelnuts or glacé (candied) cherries, to decorate

Any fresh or drained canned fruit, to serve

1 Whip the cream and fold in the chocolate spread and brandy, sherry, rum or whisky.

2 Spoon into the chocolate cups and swirl the tops with a teaspoon. Alternatively, put the mixture into a piping bag and pipe it into the cases.

3 Sprinkle with chopped nuts or top each with a halved glacé cherry. Chill until ready to serve.

4 Place on serving plates and arrange slices of fruit attractively at the side of each cup.

PREPARATION TIME:
5 MINUTES
PLUS CHILLING TIME

Almost Tiramisu

SERVES 6	METRIC	IMPERIAL	AMERICAN
Trifle sponges	4	4	4
Strong black coffee	150 ml	¼ pt	⅔ cup
Packet of egg custard (or crème caramel) mix	1	1	1
Milk	450 ml	¾ pt	2 cups
Brandy or coffee liqueur	15–30 ml	1–2 tbsp	1–2 tbsp
Whipped cream	150 ml	¼ pt	⅔ cup
Drinking (sweetened) chocolate powder	15 ml	1 tbsp	1 tbsp

1 Break up the sponges and place in a shallow round glass dish.

2 Add the coffee and leave to soak.

3 Make up the egg custard or crème caramel mix with the milk. Leave to cool slightly, then stir in the brandy or coffee liqueur.

4 Carefully pour over the sponge and chill until set.

5 Cover with the whipped cream and dust with chocolate powder.

PREPARATION TIME:
10 MINUTES
PLUS CHILLING TIME

Note: If you use crème caramel mix, reserve the sachet of caramel to drizzle over yoghurt and fresh bananas to make another dessert.

Coffee Nut Delight

SERVES 3–4	METRIC	IMPERIAL	AMERICAN
Packet of egg custard (or crème caramel) mix	1	1	1
Instant coffee powder	15 ml	1 tbsp	1 tbsp
Milk	600 ml	1 pt	2½ cups
Small packet of peanut brittle	1	1	1
Thick plain yoghurt or fromage frais	150 ml	¼ pt	⅔ cup

1 Whisk the custard mix and coffee into the milk. Bring to the boil and boil for 2 minutes as directed.

2 Cool slightly, then pour into a glass serving dish. Leave to cool completely, then chill until set.

3 Put the peanut brittle in a bag and crush it with a rolling pin.

4 Just before serving, spread the yoghurt or fromage frais over the coffee custard and sprinkle with the crushed peanut brittle.

PREPARATION TIME:
5 MINUTES
PLUS CHILLING

Note: If you use crème caramel mix, drizzle the sachet of caramel over the yoghurt or fromage frais before adding the peanut brittle.

No-effort Crumble

SERVES 3–4	METRIC	IMPERIAL	AMERICAN
Can of fruit, drained with the juice reserved	410 g	14½ oz	1 large
Weetabix	2	2	2
Light brown sugar	15 ml	1 tbsp	1 tbsp
Butter or margarine, melted	50 g	2 oz	¼ cup
Ground ginger, cinnamon or mixed (apple-pie) spice	2.5 ml	½ tsp	½ tsp
Cream or custard, to serve			

1 Put the fruit in a 1 litre/1¾ pt/4¼ cup ovenproof dish.

2 Crumble the cereal and mix with the sugar, butter or margarine and spice.

3 Sprinkle over the fruit, pressing down lightly. Bake in the oven at 190°C/375°F/gas mark 5 for about 15 minutes until crisp. Serve warm with cream or custard.

PREPARATION TIME: 3 MINUTES COOKING TIME: 15 MINUTES

Peach and Raisin Crisp

SERVES 6	METRIC	IMPERIAL	AMERICAN
Cans peach slices, drained with the juice reserved	2×400 g	2×14 oz	2 large
Raisins	75 g	3 oz	½ cup
Margarine	25 g	1 oz	2 tbsp
Plain (all-purpose) flour	50 g	2 oz	½ cup
Caster (superfine) sugar	25 g	1 oz	2 tbsp
Original Oat Crunch cereal	100 g	4 oz	1 cup
Custard, to serve			

1 Put the fruit in the base of a 1.2 litre/2 pt/5 cup ovenproof dish. Sprinkle the raisins over.

2 Rub the margarine into the flour until the mixture resembles breadcrumbs. Stir in the sugar and Original Oat Crunch. Spoon the crumble over the fruit and press down lightly.

3 Bake in the oven at 190°C/375°F/gas mark 5 for about 35 minutes until golden and crisp. Serve hot with custard and the reserved juice.

PREPARATION TIME:
5 MINUTES

COOKING TIME:
35 MINUTES

Apricot and Ginger Flan

SERVES 4	METRIC	IMPERIAL	AMERICAN
Gingernut biscuits (cookies), crushed	175 g	6 oz	6 oz
Butter, melted	50 g	2 oz	¼ cup
Can of apricot pie filling	½	½	½
Can of evaporated milk, chilled	175 g	6 oz	1 small
Glacé (candied) cherries and angelica leaves, to decorate			

⌘

1 Mix the biscuit crumbs with the butter and press into the base and sides of an 18 cm/7 in flan dish (pie pan). Chill until firm.

2 Sieve (strain) or liquidise the pie filling to form a smooth purée.

3 Whip the evaporated milk until thick and fluffy. Gradually whisk in the purée and spoon it into the flan case (pie shell).

4 Decorate with cherries and angelica and chill until ready to serve.

PREPARATION TIME:
10 MINUTES
PLUS CHILLING TIME

Note: To make another dessert, purée the remaining pie filling, then heat it through with 15 ml/1 tbsp orange liqueur or apricot brandy and serve spooned over vanilla ice cream.

Apricot Nut Crunch

SERVES 6	METRIC	IMPERIAL	AMERICAN
Can of apricots	410 g	14½ oz	1 large
Orange jelly (jello) tablet	1	1	1
Butter	25 g	1 oz	2 tbsp
Golden (light corn) syrup	15 ml	1 tbsp	1 tbsp
Chopped nuts	15 ml	1 tbsp	1 tbsp
Corn or bran flakes, lightly crushed	50 g	2 oz	2 cups
Thick plain yoghurt or whipped cream	150 ml	¼ pt	⅔ cup

1 Drain the fruit, reserving the juice. Pass it through a sieve (strainer) or purée the fruit in a blender or food processor.

2 Make the juice up to 450 ml/¾ pt/2 cups with water. Heat a little of this liquid, add the jelly tablet and stir until dissolved. Stir in the remainder of the liquid.

3 Stir in the fruit purée and turn into a glass dish. Chill until set.

4 Melt the butter with the syrup. Add the nuts and cereal. Mix gently. Spread the yoghurt or cream on top of the apricots. Top with the cereal mixture and chill again until ready to serve.

PREPARATION TIME:
10 MINUTES
PLUS CHILLING TIME

Black Forest Rice

SERVES 4	METRIC	IMPERIAL	AMERICAN
Can of cherry pie filling	410 g	14½ oz	1 large
Can of chocolate rice pudding	425 g	15 oz	1 large
Can of cream	170 g	6 oz	1 small

Grated chocolate or drinking (sweetened) chocolate powder, to decorate

1 Layer the cherry pie filling and chocolate rice in four glasses.

2 Drain the whey off the cream and pipe or spoon a swirl of cream on top of each.

3 Sprinkle with grated chocolate or drinking chocolate powder. Chill, if time, before serving.

PREPARATION TIME:
3 MINUTES

Raspberry Baked Alaska

SERVES 4	METRIC	IMPERIAL	AMERICAN
Jam Swiss (jelly) roll	1	1	1
Egg whites	3	3	3
Caster (superfine) sugar	175 g	6 oz	¾ cup
Scoops raspberry ripple ice cream	8	8	8
Glacé (candied) cherries and angelica leaves, to decorate	6	6	6

1 Slice the Swiss roll and arrange in a single layer on an ovenproof plate.

2 Whisk the egg whites until stiff. Whisk in half the sugar and continue whisking until stiff and glossy. Fold in the remaining sugar with a metal spoon.

3 Just before serving, pile the ice cream in a mound on top of the Swiss roll. Cover completely with the meringue mixture. Decorate with cherries and angelica and bake in the oven at 230°C/450°F/gas mark 8 for 2 minutes until the meringue is just turning golden. Serve immediately.

PREPARATION TIME:
5 MINUTES

COOKING TIME:
2 MINUTES

Rhubarb and Custard Charlotte

SERVES 4–5	METRIC	IMPERIAL	AMERICAN
Butter, melted	25 g	1 oz	2 tbsp
Slices of bread and butter, crusts removed	4	4	4
Individual carton of custard	1	1	1
Can of rhubarb, drained with the juice reserved	550 g	1 lb 4 oz	1 large
Light brown sugar	30 ml	2 tbsp	2 tbsp

1 Grease a 1.2 litre/2 pt/5 cup ovenproof dish with half the melted butter.

2 Line the dish with 2½ slices of the bread.

3 Spread the custard in the base, then top with the drained fruit.

4 Dice the remaining bread, toss in the remaining melted butter and the sugar and spoon over.

5 Bake in the oven at 200°C/400°F/gas mark 6 for about 40 minutes until golden. Serve with the reserved juice.

PREPARATION TIME: 5 MINUTES

COOKING TIME: 40 MINUTES

Pineapple Floating Islands

Use all milk instead of a mixture of milk and cream, if you prefer.

SERVES 4	METRIC	IMPERIAL	AMERICAN
Butter	50 g	2 oz	¼ cup
Caster (superfine) sugar	100 g	4 oz	½ cup
Cornflour (cornstarch)	25 g	1 oz	¼ cup
Milk	300 ml	½ pt	1¼ cups
Single (light) cream	150 ml	¼ pt	⅔ cup
Can of crushed pineapple, drained with the juice reserved	440 g	15½ oz	1 large
Eggs, separated	4 large	4 large	4 large

1 Beat the butter and half the sugar until light and fluffy. Blend in the cornflour.

2 Warm the milk and cream together but do not boil. Pour on to the creamed mixture. Return to the pan and cook, stirring, until thickened.

3 Put the crushed pineapple in the base of a 1.5 litre/2½ pt/6 cup ovenproof dish. Pour the custard over.

4 Whisk the egg whites until stiff, add 40 g/1½ oz/3 tbsp of the sugar and whisk again until glossy. Put four spoonfuls of the meringue on top of the custard to make the 'islands' and sprinkle with the remaining sugar.

5 Bake in the oven at 150°C/300°F/gas mark 2 for 30 minutes or until the meringues are light and golden. Serve hot or cold with the reserved pineapple juice.

PREPARATION TIME:
8 MINUTES

COOKING TIME:
30 MINUTES

Chocolate Lemon Flan

SERVES 4–6	METRIC	IMPERIAL	AMERICAN
Chocolate digestive biscuits (Graham crackers), crushed	225 g	8 oz	8 oz
Butter, melted	100 g	4 oz	½ cup
Double (heavy) or whipping cream	150 ml	¼ pt	⅔ cup
Can of sweetened condensed milk	200 g	7 oz	1 small
Lemon juice	90 ml	6 tbsp	6 tbsp
Grated chocolate, to decorate			

1 Mix the biscuit crumbs with the butter and press into the base and sides of a 20 cm/8 in flan dish (pie pan). Chill until firm.

2 Whip the cream until softly peaking. Fold in the condensed milk and lemon juice. Turn into the flan case (pie shell). Chill, preferably overnight, then decorate with grated chocolate before serving.

PREPARATION TIME:
5 MINUTES
PLUS CHILLING TIME

Pineapple Upside-down Pudding

SERVES 6	METRIC	IMPERIAL	AMERICAN
Butter	15 g	½ oz	1 tbsp
Light brown sugar	30 ml	2 tbsp	2 tbsp
Can of pineapple slices, drained with the juice reserved	225 g	8 oz	1 small
Glacé (candied) cherries, halved			
Angelica leaves			
Packet of sponge cake mix	1	1	1
Egg and water, according to packet directions			

1 Liberally butter a 10 cm/8 in round sandwich tin (pan) or other ovenproof dish.

2 Sprinkle the sugar over the base, then top with the pineapple rings.

3 Place a halved glacé cherry, cut side up, in the centre of each ring. Decorate the gaps between the pineapple rings with angelica leaves and more halved cherries.

4 Make up the sponge mixture according to the packet directions. Spoon over the fruit.

5 Bake in the oven at 190°C/375°F/gas mark 5 for 20 minutes until risen and the centre springs back when pressed.

6 Leave to cool slightly in the tin, then loosen round the edges and turn out on to a serving plate. Serve with the juice.

PREPARATION TIME: 8 MINUTES

COOKING TIME: 20 MINUTES

No-fuss Bakewell Tart

Not quite as good as a traditional one from Bakewell, but an excellent sweet all the same!

SERVES 6	METRIC	IMPERIAL	AMERICAN
Shortcrust pastry (basic pie crust)	175 g	6 oz	6 oz
Raspberry jam (conserve)	30–45 ml	2–3 tbsp	2–3 tbsp
Packet of sponge cake mix	1	1	1
Egg and water, according to packet directions			
A little almond essence (extract)			
Flaked (slivered) almonds	15 ml	1 tbsp	1 tbsp

1 Roll out the pastry and use to line a 10 cm/8 in flan dish (pie pan) set on a baking sheet.

2 Spread the jam over the base.

3 Make up the sponge according to the packet directions, adding a few drops of almond essence. Spread over the jam. Scatter with almonds.

4 Bake for 20–30 minutes at 190°C/375°F/gas mark 5 until the pastry is cooked and the sponge springs back when pressed. Serve warm or cold.

PREPARATION TIME:
8 MINUTES

COOKING TIME:
20–30 MINUTES

Crêpes Suzette

SERVES 4	METRIC	IMPERIAL	AMERICAN
Packet of batter mix (made into 8 pancakes as directed)	*1*	*1*	*1*
Butter	*25 g*	*1 oz*	*2 tbsp*
Light brown sugar	*45 ml*	*3 tbsp*	*3 tbsp*
Orange juice	*60 ml*	*4 tbsp*	*4 tbsp*
Lemon juice	*15 ml*	*1 tbsp*	*1 tbsp*
Orange liqueur or brandy	*45 ml*	*3 tbsp*	*3 tbsp*

1 Melt the butter in a large frying pan (skillet). Add the sugar and stir over a gentle heat until the sugar dissolves.

2 Add the fruit juices. Stir well for about 3–4 minutes to dissolve the caramel.

3 Fold the pancakes into quarters. Place one in the pan, spoon over the juices, then push to one side. Continue until all the pancakes are in the pan and bathed in juices.

4 Pour over the liqueur or brandy, set alight straight away and shake the pan until the flames subside. Serve hot.

PREPARATION TIME:
7 MINUTES

COOKING TIME:
10 MINUTES
PLUS PANCAKE
COOKING TIME

Variation: Try spreading pancakes with a little cream cheese, then folding and heating in the pan with a can of cherry pie filling and a dash of water and lemon juice. Flambé with a little cherry brandy or kirsch.

Pear and Chocolate Rolls

SERVES 6	METRIC	IMPERIAL	AMERICAN
Can of pears, drained with the juice reserved	410 g	14½ oz	1 large
Chocolate chips	50 g	2 oz	½ cup
Filo pastry (paste) sheets	6	6	6
Melted butter for brushing			
Cocoa (unsweetened chocolate) powder	15 ml	1 tbsp	1 tbsp
Cornflour (cornstarch)	15 ml	1 tbsp	1 tbsp
Caster (superfine) sugar, to taste			

1 Chop the pears and mix with the chocolate chips.

2 Lay a filo sheet on a board. Brush with a little melted butter. Fold in half and brush lightly again.

3 Spoon a sixth of the pear mixture along the centre of one long edge. Fold in the sides, then roll up. Place on a buttered baking sheet. Brush lightly with butter.

4 Repeat with the remaining pastry and filling.

5 Bake in the oven at 200°C/400°F/gas mark 6 for about 15 minutes or until golden.

6 Meanwhile, make the sauce. Make the reserved pear juice up to 300 ml/½ pt/1¼ cups with water. Blend a little with the cocoa and cornflour in a saucepan. Stir in the remainder. Bring to the boil and cook for 2 minutes until thickened. Sweeten to taste with sugar.

7 Serve hot with the chocolate sauce spooned over.

PREPARATION TIME:
15 MINUTES

COOKING TIME:
15 MINUTES

Pear and Cinnamon Clafoutie

SERVES 4–6	METRIC	IMPERIAL	AMERICAN
Can of pears, drained with the juice reserved	410 g	14½ oz	1 large
Butter for greasing			
Packet of batter mix	1	1	1
Egg, according to packet directions			
Milk or water, according to packet directions			
Ground cinnamon	5 ml	1 tsp	1 tsp
Icing (confectioners') sugar for dusting			

1 Lay the pears in a buttered shallow ovenproof dish.

2 Make up the batter according to the packet directions. Pour over. Sprinkle with the cinnamon.

3 Bake in the oven at 200°C/400°F/gas mark 6 for about 30 minutes until risen and golden. Dust with sifted icing sugar before serving with the juice.

PREPARATION TIME: 6 MINUTES COOKING TIME: ABOUT 30 MINUTES

Speedy Strawberry Cheesecake

Ring the changes with other pie fillings for toppings.

SERVES 6	METRIC	IMPERIAL	AMERICAN
Sponge flan case (pie shell)	23 cm	9 in	9 in
Low-fat soft cheese	200 g	7 oz	scant 1 cup
Caster (superfine) sugar	50 g	2 oz	¼ cup
Vanilla essence (extract)	2.5 ml	½ tsp	½ tsp
Whipped cream	150 ml	¼ pt	⅔ cup
Can of strawberry pie filling	425 g	15 oz	1 large

1 Put the flan case on a serving plate.

2 Beat the cheese with the sugar and vanilla, then fold in the whipped cream.

3 Spoon into the flan case and spread evenly. Chill until fairly firm.

4 Spread the pie filling over and, if time allows, chill again before serving.

PREPARATION TIME:
3 MINUTES
PLUS CHILLING TIME

SNACKS AND LIGHT MEALS

✳

Are you always grabbing a quick bite to eat

because time is short? You may not want a

full-blown meal, but that doesn't mean the

food can't be tasty and satisfying. Try

slitting open some pitta breads, spreading the

inside with brown sauce and filling with hot

baked beans before sprinkling with grated

cheese and warming under the grill (broiler)

or in the microwave; frying a cheese and

onion ring sandwich until golden and

melting; or mashing a couple of chopped

pickled onions into grated cheese before

grilling on thick, buttered slices of bread

Now read on ...

Pizza Rolls

SERVES 4	METRIC	IMPERIAL	AMERICAN
Soft rolls	4	4	4
Can of chopped tomatoes, drained	225 g	8 oz	1 small
Dried oregano	5 ml	1 tsp	1 tsp
Mozzarella or Cheddar cheese, grated	100 g	4 oz	1 cup

1 Cut a shallow slit in the top of each roll.

2 Gently pull away some of the soft filling to leave a thick shell.

3 Divide the tomatoes between the rolls. Sprinkle with the herbs and top with cheese.

4 Wrap each roll in foil and steam in a steamer or colander over a saucepan of boiling water for 10 minutes until the cheese has melted. Alternatively, bake in the oven at 220°C/425°F/gas mark 7 for 10 minutes.

PREPARATION TIME: 3 MINUTES COOKING TIME: 10 MINUTES

Note: You can heat these Pizza Rolls in the microwave. Put them in a microwave-safe dish with a lid. Do not wrap in foil. Microwave for 2 minutes, then rearrange and cook a little longer, depending on the power output of your model. Do not overcook or they will be tough.

Quick Pan Pizza

SERVES 1–2	METRIC	IMPERIAL	AMERICAN
Self-raising (self-rising) flour	100 g	4 oz	1 cup
Pinch of salt			
Oil	45 ml	3 tbsp	3 tbsp
Can of chopped tomatoes, drained	225 g	8 oz	1 small
Dried oregano	1.5 ml	¼ tsp	¼ tsp
Cheddar or Mozzarella cheese, grated	50 g	2 oz	½ cup

Additional topping suggestions: chopped ham, sliced mushrooms, drained sweetcorn (corn), diced (bell) pepper, pepperoni, drained pineapple pieces

1 Mix the flour with the salt and 30 ml/2 tbsp of the oil in a bowl. Add enough cold water to form a soft but not sticky dough.

2 Knead gently, then flatten out to a round to fit the base of a frying pan (skillet).

3 Heat the remaining oil in the pan, add the dough and fry (sauté) for about 3 minutes until golden brown underneath. Turn over.

4 Spread the tomatoes over, sprinkle with the herbs, add any other chosen topping, then sprinkle with the cheese.

5 Fry for 2–3 minutes, then place the pan under a hot grill (broiler) and cook until the cheese is melted and bubbling. Serve hot.

PREPARATION TIME:
5 MINUTES

COOKING TIME:
8 MINUTES

Salmon Tartare Sandwiches

MAKES 4 ROUNDS	METRIC	IMPERIAL	AMERICAN
Butter or margarine	75 g	3 oz	⅓ cup
Can of pink salmon	100 g	4 oz	1 small
Tartare sauce	30 ml	2 tbsp	2 tbsp
Chopped parsley	15 ml	1 tbsp	1 tbsp
Salt and pepper			
Slices of bread	8	8	8

1 Put the butter in a bowl and mash with a fork.

2 Discard the bones and skin and mash the fish into the butter with the tartare sauce, parsley and a little salt and pepper.

3 Spread over the slices of bread and sandwich together in pairs. Cut off the crusts, if preferred. Cut into triangles and serve.

PREPARATION TIME:
5 MINUTES

Orange and Cream Cheese Deckers

MAKES 3 ROUNDS	METRIC	IMPERIAL	AMERICAN
Slices of bread	6	6	6
Low-fat soft cheese	200 g	7 oz	scant 1 cup
Can of mandarin oranges, drained	300 g	11 oz	1 small
A little cress or shredded lettuce			
Black pepper			

1 Spread the bread with the cheese.

2 Top half the slices with the oranges, then cress or shredded lettuce leaves.

3 Season with pepper, then sandwich together with the remaining bread slices. Cut and serve.

PREPARATION TIME:
3 MINUTES

Eggy Baguette

SERVES 1–2	METRIC	IMPERIAL	AMERICAN
Small French stick	1	1	1
Butter for spreading			
Eggs	2	2	2
Dried mixed herbs	1.5 ml	¼ tsp	¼ tsp
Salt and pepper			

❋

1 Warm the French stick either in the oven, under the grill (broiler) turning frequently or in the microwave (not too long!). Cut a slit along the length and butter inside.

2 Meanwhile, beat the eggs and add 30 ml/2 tbsp water, the herbs and some salt and pepper. Beat well.

3 Heat an omelette pan and add a knob of butter. When sizzling, pour in the egg mixture. Lift and stir the egg until set. Fold into three.

4 Slide inside the French stick and cut in half, if preferred.

PREPARATION TIME:
5 MINUTES

Waffle Dagwoods

SERVES 2	METRIC	IMPERIAL	AMERICAN
Frozen potato waffles	4	4	4
Eggs	2	2	2
Butter or oil for shallow-frying			
Ham slices	2	2	2
A little shredded lettuce			

1 Grill (broil) or fry (sauté) the waffles according to the packet directions.

2 Fry the eggs in a little butter or oil until cooked.

3 Place the slices of ham on two waffles. Top each with an egg and some shredded lettuce. Finish with the second waffle and try to eat!

PREPARATION TIME:
2 MINUTES

COOKING TIME:
ABOUT 6 MINUTES

Fish Fingers American-style

SERVES 2	METRIC	IMPERIAL	AMERICAN
Fish fingers	8	8	8
Soft baps	2	2	2
Processed cheese slices	2	2	2
Tartare sauce	30 ml	2 tbsp	2 tbsp
A little shredded lettuce			

1 Grill (broil), fry (sauté) or microwave the fish fingers.

2 Split the rolls and lay four fish fingers in each roll.

3 Top each with a slice of cheese and flash under a hot grill (broiler) to melt the cheese.

4 Add tartare sauce, shredded lettuce and then close the lids of the rolls. Serve.

PREPARATION TIME:
2 MINUTES

COOKING TIME:
UP TO 8 MINUTES

Pitta Pocket

SERVES 1	METRIC	IMPERIAL	AMERICAN
Pitta bread	1	1	1
Shredded lettuce	15 ml	1 tbsp	1 tbsp
Tomato slices	2	2	2
Cucumber slices	2	2	2
Filling suggestions: a little tuna, chopped ham, mashed pilchard, sliced corned beef, chopped frankfurter, salami or hard-boiled (hard-cooked) egg			
Mayonnaise	10 ml	2 tsp	2 tsp

1 Toast or microwave the pitta just enough to puff up. Split along one edge to form a pocket.

2 Add the shredded lettuce, tomato and cucumber and any other suggested filling. Finish with the mayonnaise.

PREPARATION TIME:
4 MINUTES

Cheese and Mushroom Croissants

If you buy ready-split croissants, they can be used straight from the freezer.

SERVES 2–4	METRIC	IMPERIAL	AMERICAN
Croissants	4	4	4
Can of creamed mushrooms	215 g	7½ oz	1 small
Cheddar cheese, grated	50 g	2 oz	½ cup

1 Carefully open the croissants at the split, without breaking apart, or make a slit in each if necessary.

2 Spread the creamed mushrooms inside and pack in the cheese.

3 Grill (broil), turning once, until the cheese has melted, and the croissants are crisp and hot through. Take care not to burn. Alternatively heat as for Pizza Rolls (page 131).

PREPARATION TIME:
2 MINUTES

COOKING TIME:
5 MINUTES

Naan Tiffin

SERVES 4	METRIC	IMPERIAL	AMERICAN
Naan breads	2	2	2
Can of pease pudding	225 g	8 oz	1 small
Curry paste	10 ml	2 tsp	2 tsp
Mango chutney	30 ml	2 tbsp	2 tbsp
Lemon juice, to taste			
A little shredded lettuce (optional)			

1 Grill (broil) or microwave the naans according to the packet directions.

2 Heat the pease pudding with the curry paste in a saucepan or the microwave until hot through, stirring occasionally.

3 Spread the pease pudding mixture over the surface of the naans.

4 Spread the mango chutney over and sprinkle with lemon juice. Add shredded lettuce, if liked.

5 Fold in halves, then cut into handy-sized wedges.

6 Wrap in kitchen paper and eat in your fingers.

PREPARATION TIME:
2 MINUTES

COOKING TIME:
3 MINUTES

TEATIME TREATS

We tend to think that teatime with cups of tea, bread, jam, cakes and biscuits is a thing of the past. Yet how many of us love a little something with our mid-afternoon cuppa? When we have guests to lunch on Sundays, it still seems appropriate to provide a snack at teatime and, as I seldom think about it in advance, it's got to be something quick knocked up from the store cupboard.

No-bake Crunchy Bars

These are ideal for lunch boxes too.

MAKES 12–16	METRIC	IMPERIAL	AMERICAN
Butter or margarine	175 g	6 oz	¾ cup
Light brown sugar	50 g	2 oz	¼ cup
Golden (light corn) syrup	30 ml	2 tbsp	2 tbsp
Cocoa (unsweetened chocolate) powder	45 ml	3 tbsp	3 tbsp
Raisins	75 g	3 oz	½ cup
Original Oat Crunch cereal	350 g	12 oz	3 cups
Plain (semi-sweet) chocolate	225 g	8 oz	8 oz

1 Oil the base of an 18×28 cm/7×11 in baking tin (pan) and line with baking parchment.

2 Melt the butter or margarine, sugar, syrup and cocoa in a pan. Stir in the raisins and cereal. Press into the tin.

3 Melt the chocolate in a pan over hot water or in the microwave and spread over, right to the corners.

4 Chill until set, cut into fingers and store in an airtight tin.

PREPARATION TIME:
ABOUT 5 MINUTES
PLUS CHILLING TIME

Quick Rum Truffles

MAKES 12	METRIC	IMPERIAL	AMERICAN
Chocolate hazelnut spread	30 ml	2 tbsp	2 tbsp
Cake crumbs	50 g	2 oz	½ cup
Rum, brandy or sherry essence (extract)	5 ml	1 tsp	1 tsp
Cocoa (unsweetened chocolate) powder or chocolate vermicelli, to coat			

1 Mix the chocolate spread and cake crumbs together until well blended.

2 Add the essence to taste and a little water to give a soft but not sticky consistency.

3 Roll the mixture into small balls, then roll in cocoa or vermicelli. Place in small paper cases (candy cups) and chill.

PREPARATION TIME:
10 MINUTES
PLUS CHILLING TIME

The Easiest Flapjacks

MAKES 12	METRIC	IMPERIAL	AMERICAN
Butter or margarine, softened	*75 g*	*3 oz*	*⅓ cup*
Light brown sugar	*75 g*	*3 oz*	*⅓ cup*
Rolled oats	*100 g*	*4 oz*	*1 cup*
Mixed (apple-pie) spice (optional)	*5 ml*	*1 tsp*	*1 tsp*

1 Beat the butter or margarine in a bowl until creamy.

2 Add the sugar, oats and spice, if using, and work in until well mixed.

3 Turn into a greased 18 cm/7 in square tin (pan) and press down well. Bake in the oven at 220°C/425°F/ gas mark 7 for 15–20 minutes until golden.

4 Allow to cool in the tin for 10 minutes, then cut into pieces. Leave in the tin until cold before removing.

PREPARATION TIME:
3 MINUTES

COOKING TIME:
15–20 MINUTES

Cinnamon French Toast

SERVES 4	METRIC	IMPERIAL	AMERICAN
Egg	1	1	1
Milk	30 ml	2 tbsp	2 tbsp
Thick slices of white bread, crusts removed	4	4	4
Butter	25 g	1 oz	2 tbsp
Oil	30 ml	2 tbsp	2 tbsp
Caster (superfine) sugar	20 ml	4 tsp	4 tsp
Ground cinnamon	5 ml	1 tsp	1 tsp

1 Beat the egg and milk together. Dip the bread in to coat completely.

2 Heat the butter and oil in a large frying pan (skillet). Fry (sauté) the slices for about 1½ minutes on each side over a high heat until a deep golden brown.

3 Drain on kitchen paper.

4 Mix the sugar and cinnamon on a flat plate. Dip the bread in the mixture until coated on both sides. Serve straight away cut into triangles.

PREPARATION TIME: 2 MINUTES

COOKING TIME: 3 MINUTES

Chewy Apricot Bars

MAKES 15	METRIC	IMPERIAL	AMERICAN
Can of evaporated milk	175 g	6 oz	1 small
Clear honey	20 ml	4 tsp	4 tsp
Apple juice	45 ml	3 tbsp	3 tbsp
Butter	50 g	2 oz	¼ cup
Light brown sugar	50 g	2 oz	¼ cup
Sultanas (golden raisins)	50 g	2 oz	⅓ cup
Ready-to-eat dried apricots, chopped	225 g	8 oz	1⅓ cups
Desiccated (shredded) coconut	100 g	4 oz	1 cup
Rolled oats	225 g	8 oz	2 cups

1 Grease a 28×18 cm/11×7 in baking tin (pan).

2 Heat the evaporated milk with the honey, apple juice, butter and sugar until melted.

3 Add the remaining ingredients and mix well. Press into the tin.

4 Wrap in clingfilm (plastic wrap) and chill overnight to allow the flavours to develop before cutting into bars.

PREPARATION TIME:
5 MINUTES
PLUS CHILLING TIME

Fruit and Fibre Crackles

MAKES 15	METRIC	IMPERIAL	AMERICAN
Plain (semi-sweet) chocolate	100 g	4 oz	4 oz
Butter or margarine	50 g	2 oz	¼ cup
Golden (light corn) syrup	15 ml	1 tbsp	1 tbsp
Fruit and Fibre breakfast cereal	100 g	4 oz	2 cups

1 Melt the chocolate in a bowl over a pan of hot water or in the microwave.

2 Beat in the butter or margarine and syrup until smooth, heating a little more if necessary.

3 Stir in the cereal until completely coated. Pack into paper cases (cupcake papers) and chill until firm.

PREPARATION TIME:
5 MINUTES
PLUS SETTING TIME

Peanut Bites

MAKES 18	METRIC	IMPERIAL	AMERICAN
Plain biscuit (cookie) crumbs	225 g	8 oz	2 cups
Butter, melted	100 g	4 oz	½ cup
Crunchy peanut butter	225 g	8 oz	1 cup
Glacé (candied) cherries, chopped	25 g	1 oz	1 oz
Currants	25 g	1 oz	3 tbsp

1 Mix together all the ingredients until well blended.

2 Press into a greased 28×18 cm/11×7 in baking tin (pan). Cover with foil or clingfilm (plastic wrap) and chill until firm before cutting into squares.

PREPARATION TIME:
4 MINUTES
PLUS CHILLING TIME

Raspberry Oat Squares

MAKES 15	METRIC	IMPERIAL	AMERICAN
Self-raising (self-rising) flour	225 g	8 oz	2 cups
Salt	5 ml	1 tsp	1 tsp
Margarine	175 g	6 oz	¾ cup
Rolled oats	175 g	6 oz	1½ cups
Caster (superfine) sugar	175 g	6 oz	¾ cup
Can of raspberries	300 g	11 oz	1 small

1 Put the flour and salt in a bowl. Rub in the margarine, then stir in the oats and sugar.

2 Grease a 28×18 cm/11×7 in baking tin (pan) and press half the mixture into the base.

3 Drain the raspberries and scatter the fruit over the top.

4 Cover with remaining crumble mixture, pressing down well.

5 Bake in the oven at 200°C/400°F/gas mark 6 for 30 minutes. Leave to cool for 15 minutes, then cut into squares and transfer to a wire rack to cool completely.

PREPARATION TIME:
8 MINUTES

COOKING TIME:
30 MINUTES
PLUS COOLING TIME

Broken Biscuit Cakes

You can buy packets of broken biscuits very cheaply or use up the dregs of the biscuit barrel.

MAKES 15	METRIC	IMPERIAL	AMERICAN
Butter or margarine	100 g	4 oz	½ cup
Caster (superfine) sugar	15 ml	1 tbsp	1 tbsp
Golden (light corn) syrup	15 ml	1 tbsp	1 tbsp
Cocoa (unsweetened chocolate) powder	30 ml	2 tbsp	2 tbsp
Broken biscuits (cookies), crushed	225 g	8 oz	2 cups
Sultanas (golden raisins)	50 g	2 oz	⅓ cup

1 Melt the fat, sugar, syrup and cocoa in a saucepan until well blended, but do not boil.

2 Stir in the biscuits and sultanas.

3 Press into a greased 28 × 18 cm/11 × 7 in baking tin (pan). Chill until firm, then cut into squares.

PREPARATION TIME:
3 MINUTES

COOKING TIME:
2 MINUTES
PLUS CHILLING TIME

SAUCES AND SAVOURY BUTTERS

Sauces and savoury butters can spice up plain chops or fish fillets from your freezer or brighten a boring can of anything from tuna to frankfurters.

Quick Tomato Sauce

Use for everything from pasta to pork chops. When you're in a desperate hurry, just use passata straight from the jar, seasoned, if you like, with a little garlic purée (paste), granules or the real thing, and a pinch of dried oregano or basil.

SERVES 4	METRIC	IMPERIAL	AMERICAN
Onion, chopped	1	1	1
Oil	15 ml	1 tbsp	1 tbsp
Can of chopped tomatoes	400 g	14 oz	1 large
Tomato purée (paste)	15 ml	1 tbsp	1 tbsp
Salt and pepper			
Dried oregano or basil	2.5 ml	½ tsp	½ tsp

1 Fry (sauté) the onion in the oil for 2 minutes to soften.

2 Add the remaining ingredients, bring to the boil and simmer for 10 minutes until pulpy. Use as required.

PREPARATION TIME:
3 MINUTES

COOKING TIME:
12 MINUTES

All-purpose Barbecue Sauce

Use as a side sauce with grills or barbecues, or as a basting mixture for chops, chicken or fish.

SERVES 4	METRIC	IMPERIAL	AMERICAN
Lemon juice	15 ml	1 tbsp	1 tbsp
Red wine or other vinegar	15 ml	1 tbsp	1 tbsp
Tomato ketchup (catsup)	30 ml	2 tbsp	2 tbsp
Worcestershire sauce	15 ml	1 tbsp	1 tbsp
Golden (light corn) syrup	30 ml	2 tbsp	2 tbsp

1 Mix together all the ingredients until thoroughly blended.

2 Store in a screw-topped jar in the fridge for up to 1 month.

PREPARATION TIME:
3 MINUTES

Garlic and Herb Sauce

Serve with fish, vegetables or white meat.

SERVES 4	METRIC	IMPERIAL	AMERICAN
Cornflour (cornstarch)	15 ml	1 tbsp	1 tbsp
Milk	300 ml	½ pt	1¼ cups
Butter or margarine	15 g	½ oz	1 tbsp
Garlic and herb soft cheese	90 g	3½ oz	scant ½ cup

Salt and pepper

1 Whisk the cornflour with a little of the milk in a saucepan until smooth. Stir in the remaining milk. Add the butter or margarine.

2 Bring to the boil, stirring until thickened.

3 Add the cheese, cut into pieces, and continue stirring over a gentle heat until blended. Season with salt and pepper and use as required.

PREPARATION TIME: 2 MINUTES

COOKING TIME: 4 MINUTES

Gran's Salad Dressing

Use as an alternative to mayonnaise for everything from coleslaw to beetroot.

SERVES 4–6	METRIC	IMPERIAL	AMERICAN
Light brown sugar	15 ml	1 tbsp	1 tbsp
Made English mustard	5 ml	1 tsp	1 tsp
Single (light) cream or evaporated milk	150 ml	¼ pt	⅔ cup
Malt vinegar, to taste			
Salt and pepper			

1 Mix together the sugar, mustard and cream or evaporated milk until the sugar dissolves.

2 Whisk in vinegar to taste. Season with salt and pepper. Store in a screw-topped jar in the fridge for up to 2 weeks.

PREPARATION TIME:
3 MINUTES

Stroganoff Sauce

Use with stir-fry meats or fillets of fish.

SERVES 4	METRIC	IMPERIAL	AMERICAN
Onion, finely chopped	1	1	1
Butter	15 g	½ oz	1 tbsp
Brandy	15 ml	1 tbsp	1 tbsp
Cornflour (cornstarch)	20 ml	4 tsp	4 tsp
Milk	300 ml	½ pt	1¼ cups
Soft cheese with black pepper	90 g	3½ oz	scant ½ cup
Salt			
Chopped parsley	15 ml	1 tbsp	1 tbsp

1 Fry (sauté) the onion gently in the butter for 3 minutes until soft but not browned.

2 Blend the brandy with the cornflour and a little of the milk. Stir in the remaining milk and add to the pan. Bring to the boil, stirring until thickened.

3 Add the cheese in small pieces and continue stirring over a gentle heat until blended. Season with salt. Add the parsley. Use as required.

PREPARATION TIME:
2 MINUTES

COOKING TIME:
6 MINUTES

Garlic Butter

FILLS 1 SMALL FRENCH STICK	METRIC	IMPERIAL	AMERICAN
Garlic clove, crushed	1	1	1
OR garlic purée (paste) or granules	5 ml	1 tsp	1 tsp
Butter, softened	75 g	3 oz	⅓ cup
Black pepper			

1 Mash the garlic into the butter and add a good grinding of pepper.

2 Spread in French bread (or rolls), wrap in foil and bake until crisp and melted. Alternatively, shape into a roll on a piece of baking parchment, roll up and chill ready to cut into slices to top plain cooked meat or fish.

PREPARATION TIME:
2 MINUTES
PLUS CHILLING TIME

Variations
- **Garlic and herb:** Add 5 ml/1 tsp dried mixed herbs to the garlic butter and continue as above.
- **Herb:** Omit the garlic and add 10 ml/2 tsp dried mixed herbs to plain butter and continue as above.
- **Tomato:** Add 15 ml/1 tbsp tomato purée (paste) to plain or garlic butter. Mash thoroughly to mix. Continue as above.
- **Anchovy butter:** Add 10 ml/2 tsp anchovy essence (extract) to plain butter and continue as above.
- **Curry butter:** Add 5 ml/1 tsp (or to taste) curry paste to plain or garlic butter. Mash thoroughly to mix. Continue as above.

INDEX